DUAL ZONE
AIR FRYER COOKBOOK UK

1000 Days of Easy, Quick and Delicious English Recipes with Colour Pictures and European Measurements. Suitable for Beginners and Pros.

Lauren O'Sullivan

© **Text Copyright 2022 by [Lauren O'Sullivan]**

All rights reserved. No part of this guide may be reproduced in any form without permission in writing from the publisher except in the case of brief quotation embodied in critical articles or reviews.

HOW DOES THE DUAL ZONE AIR FRYER WORKS? 8
THE SIX PRE-SET COOKING PROGRAMS 8
OPERATION BUTTONS OF THE DUAL ZONE AIR FRYER 8

THE BENEFITS OF THE DUAL ZONE AIR FRYER 10

TIPS AND TRICKS FOR PERFECT USING 11

CLEANING AND MAINTENANCE OF THE DUAL ZONE AIR FRYER 12

BREAKFAST RECIPES 13
EGG AND BACON MUFFINS 14
BREAKFAST FRITTATA 14
CHEESY ONION OMELETTE 15
SAUSAGE BREAKFAST CASSEROLE 15
MUSHROOM AND SQUASH TOAST 15
BRUSSELS SPROUTS POTATO HASH 16
CINNAMON APPLE FRENCH TOAST 16
BREAKFAST STUFFED PEPPERS 17
PANCAKE DOUGHNUTS 17
MORNING PUMPKIN BREAD 17
RASPBERRY NUTELLA TOAST CUPS 18
BREAKFAST POTATOES 18
CHEESY EGG RAMEKINS 19
TURKEY HAM MUFFINS 19
SWEET POTATO HASH 19

POULTRY RECIPES 21
CHICKEN LEG BARBECUE 21
PISTACHIO CRUSTED CHICKEN 21
POPCORN CHICKEN 21
BUFFALO CHICKEN CALZONES 22
CHICKEN BURGER 22
CHICKEN SAUSAGE PIZZA 23
CHICKEN MEATBALLS 23
LEMON CHICKEN THIGHS 23
CORNISH HEN WITH ASPARAGUS 24
CORNISH HEN WITH BAKED POTATOES 24
AIR FRIED TURKEY BREAST 25
ROASTED TURKEY WITH CAULIFLOWER 25
TURKEY BURGER PATTIES 26
TARRAGON TURKEY WITH BABY POTATOES 26
TURKEY SAUSAGE WITH BRUSSELS 27

BEEF, PORK AND LAMB RECIPES 28
BEEF MEATLOAF 28
GARLIC SIRLOIN STEAK 28
BEEF KOFTA KEBAB 29
MARINATED STEAK & MUSHROOMS 29
CHEESESTEAK TAQUITOS 30
PORK CHOP WITH MUSHROOMS 30
COURGETTE PORK SKEWERS 31
PORK LETTUCE WRAPS 31
PORK CHOPS PARMIGIANA 32
SAUSAGE STUFFED COURGETTE BOATS 32
PORK SCHNITZEL 33
MINT GLAZED LEG OF LAMB 33

    Greek Lamb Burgers 34
    Mustard Lamb Chops 34
    Lemony Lamb Chops 35

FISH AND SEAFOOD RECIPES 36

    Salmon Cakes 36
    Chili Lime Tilapia 36
    Blackened Cod Fish 37
    Marinated Tuna Steaks 37
    Brown Sugar Garlic Salmon 37
    Cod Fish Nuggets 38
    Cajun Fried Catfish 38
    Coconut Shrimp 39
    Air Fried Mussels 39
    Marinated Prawns 40
    Crab Cakes 40
    Sesame Jumbo Shrimp 40
    Crab Stuffed Mushrooms 41
    Shrimp Skewers 41
    Herb Lemon Mussels 42

SIDES RECIPES 43

    Acorn Squash Slices 43
    Peppered Asparagus 43
    Green Tomato Stacks 43
    Bacon Wrapped Corn Cob 44
    Stuffed Tomatoes 44
    Garlic-Rosemary Brussels Sprouts 45
    Onion Rings 45
    Balsamic Vegetables 46
    Air-Fried Asparagus 46
    Mexican Cauliflower 47
    Air Fried Okra 47
    Breaded Summer Squash 48
    BBQ Sriracha Baby Corn 48
    Rosemary Asparagus & Potatoes 48
    Courgette With Broccoli 49

VEGAN RECIPES 50

    Carrot Fries 50
    Air Fried Mixed Vegetables 50
    Beet Chips 50
    Sweet Potatoes with Carrots 51
    Fried Mushrooms 51
    Broccoli & Squash with Peppers 52
    Sesame Kale Chips 52
    Potatoes with Green Beans 53
    Fried Patty Pan Squash 53
    Potato Chips 53
    Cinnamon Sugar Chickpeas 54
    Vegetable Chips 54
    Oregano Radishes 55
    Herb and Lemon Cauliflower 55
    Sweet Potatoes with Brussels Sprouts 55

SNACKS AND APPETIZERS RECIPES 57

    Parmesan Dill Chips 57
    Mushroom Roll-Ups 57

- Fried Ravioli 58
- Courgette Fritters 58
- Cheesy Cauliflower Tots 58
- Sweet Potato Wedges 59
- Veggie Quesadillas 59
- Kale Potato Nuggets 60
- Cheese Stuffed Mushrooms 60
- Sriracha Avocado Fries 61
- Spinach Balls 61
- Tofu Veggie Meatballs 62
- Bacon Wrapped Tater Tots 62
- Cheese Corn Fritters 63
- Jalapeno Poppers 63

DESSERTS RECIPES 64
- Blueberry Pie Egg Rolls 65
- Chocolate Chip Cookies 65
- Roasted Oranges 66
- Semolina Pudding 66
- Apple Fritters 66
- Blueberry Muffins 67
- Grilled Peaches 67
- Pecan Pie 67
- Chocolate Pudding 68
- Red Velvet Cookies 68
- Baked Stuffed Apples 69
- Brownie Muffins 69
- Scottish Shortbread Sticks 70
- Honey Lime Pineapple 70
- Chocó Lava Cake 70

COOKING CONVERSION CHART 72
.... 72

CONCLUSION 73

Introduction

The Dual Zone Air Fryer is a revolutionary kitchen appliance that cooks your favourite foods with little to no oil. This incredible kitchen tool can easily fry, bake, roast, and even dehydrate foods. Its dual-zone technology is the secret to the Dual Zone Air Fryer's success. This unique feature allows you to cook your food at two different temperature zones, giving you the perfect cook every time.
This appliance utilizes advanced cyclonic air technology to quickly circulate hot air around the food, cooking it evenly on all sides with little to no oil. This not only saves you calories, but it also reduces the amount of unhealthy fats and oils that can leach into your food.
The result is healthier, better-tasting food that is cooked evenly and efficiently. In this cookbook, we will explore some of the best recipes that can be made using the Dual Zone Air Fryer. We will also provide tips and tricks on how to get the most out of your air fryer. So, whether you want to make a quick and healthy meal or impress your guests with a gourmet dish, the Dual Zone Air Fryer Cookbook has you covered.

How Does the Dual Zone Air Fryer Works?

The Dual Zone Fryer is a new type of air fryer that claims to be able to cook food faster and more evenly than other air fryers on the market. The new 2-basket air fryer has a DUAL-ZONE technology that includes a smart finish button that cooks two food items in two different ways at the same time. It also has a MATCH function that copy the settings from the first basket to the second basket for even cooking.

The 8-quart air fryer has a capacity that can cook full family meals up to 1.8kg. The two zones have their separate baskets that cook food using cyclonic fans that heat food rapidly with circulating hot air all-around. The temperature ranges from 40°C to 240°C, and has a six pre-set cooking programs (air fry, bake, roast, dehydrate, reheat, and max crisp) that make using the air fryer even easier. We're going to discuss these cooking programs one by one below.

The Six Pre-Set Cooking Programs

The six pre-set cooking programs make it easy to cook your food. All you have to do is choose one of the pre-set cooking programs, select the right temperature, and time stated in the recipes, then the air fryer will do the rest. The programs include are:

1. Air fry: You will get the same taste of fried foods with less or without using any oil. So, if you are a fan of fried chicken, chips, or any other fried food, then this is the best mode for you as it uses up to 75% less oil than the traditional frying methods.

2. Bake: You didn't need to purchase an oven for baking different dishes. When you press the "Bake" cooking mode, the air fryer works like an oven, and you can bake different desserts like cakes, muffins, pancakes, casseroles, baked fish, and cookies, etc.

3. Roast: You can roast the chicken, vegetables, fish, beef, lamb, and pork with the help of "Roast mode cooking mode." It gives a brown texture to the food. You will get a tender and tasty meal using this roast function.

4. Max Crisp: With this cooking mode, you can cook frozen food without thawing, such as French fries, frozen chicken nuggets, frozen fish, etc. It will give crispy and tasty flavour to the food. In less time, you will get crisp and delicious food.

5. Dehydrate: You can dehydrate the vegetables, fruits, and meat, etc. You can preserve food after dehydrating for a long time. It takes several hours to cook food, but it gives you a healthy, delicious, crisp texture.

6. Reheat: If you are worried about leftover food, relax because the Dual Zone Air Fryer has a "reheat" cooking mode. You can reheat your leftover food without losing the texture and flavour of the food.

Operation Buttons of the Dual Zone Air Fryer

The Dual Zone Air Fryer has a variety of operation buttons that help the user control the temperature, cooking time, and other functions of the appliance.

Time Arrow Buttons: Using up and down arrow keys, you can easily adjust the time settings as per your recipe needs.

Temp Arrow Buttons: Using up and down arrow keys, you can easily change the temperature settings as per your recipe needs.
Sync Button: This function is used to sync the cooking time automatically and ensures that both the cooking zones finish their cooking simultaneously, even if there is a difference between their cooking times.
Match Button: This function is used to match the cooking zone 2 settings with cooking zone 1 setting on a large quantity of the same food or different food cooking at the same function, temperature, and time.
Start/Stop Button: Use this button to start the cooking process after selecting the time and temperature settings as per your recipe needs.
Standby Mode: This equipment goes into standby mode when it is powered on but not in use for more than 10 minutes.
Hold Mode: When the time setting for both zones doesn't match but you want both zones to finish cooking at the same time, the zone with the lesser time will be on hold but when the time becomes equal the hold mode will disappear and the zone on hold will start cooking. This will also show during SYNC mode if the other zone takes too long to synchronize with the rest of the zone.

The Benefits of the Dual Zone Air Fryer

The Dual Zone Air Fryer is one of the innovative product designs manufactured. Indeed, it has many features and benefits which make it a perfect choice for consumers. These includes:

Eight-Quart Capacity- The enormous 8-quart capacity, which can be divided into two sections, provides ample area for cooking both large and small amounts of food. It is ideal for cooking for large families or groups because it can accommodate a lot of food at the same time.

Multifunctional Air Fryer- This amazing dual zone air fryer with 6 pre-set functions. These functions are: air fry, max crisp, dehydrate, roast, bake, and reheat. You never need to buy separate appliances for a single cooking function.

Safer Than Deep Fryer- Traditional deep-frying method involves a large container full of sizzling oil. This can increase the safety risk of splashing hot oil over the skin. While the Dual Zone Air Fryer is close from all the sides when getting hot, there is no risk of splashing, spilling or accidental burn during the cooking process.

Smart Finish- When you put various foods in the baskets, each one takes a different amount of time to cook. When you use the smart cooking feature and start the operation, the basket with the longer cooking time will run first, while the other basket will remain on hold until the other chamber reaches the same cooking duration. Afterward, both baskets will complete the cooking process at the same time, ensuring that your food is ready to serve hot and fresh.

Match Cook- You can utilize the same cooking mode for both baskets and utilize the XL capacity with the match cook technology. By evenly cooking both dishes, you can be sure that your food will be cooked to perfection every time.

Reduce the Risk of Acrylamide Formation- Deep frying is one of the high heat cooking methods in which harmful acrylamide is formed. It is one of the causes of developing some cancer like ovarian, endometrial, oesophageal and breast cancer. On the other side, this air fryer cooks your food into very little oil and fat by circulating hot air around the food. This process lowers the risk of acrylamide formation.

Use Less Oil and Fats- The cooking basket of the oven comes with ceramic non-stick coatings and allows you to prepare your favourite food using up to 75 to 80 % less fat and oils than the traditional deep-frying method.

Wide Temperature Range- The Dual Zone Air Fryer offers a range of 105 °F to 400 °F temperature. The lower temperature range is suitable for dehydrating your favourite fruits, vegetable, and meat slices, and the higher temperature range allows you to cook thick cuts of meat.

Easy to Clean- The interior of this air fryer is made up of a non-stick coating so that you can clean it easily. The cooking tray comes in metallic and dishwasher safe, but you can easily clean it by hand if you want to.

Tips And Tricks for Perfect Using

To make sure you're using your Dual Zone Air Fryer to its fullest potential, check out these tips and tricks.
- Make sure the ingredients are laid out evenly and without overlap on the bottom of the drawer for consistent browning.
- You can alter the cooking temperature and duration at any moment. Simply choose the zone you wish to change, then use the TEMP or TIME arrows to change the temperature or the time.
- Reduce the temperature by 10°C if you're converting recipes from your normal oven.
- To prevent overcooking, periodically check your food.
- For better crispiness, insert the crisper plates according to the instructions in the user manual that came with your air fryer. The holes in the crisper plates help to circulate hot air and prevent sogginess.
- Use at least 1 tablespoon of oil when cooking fresh veggies and potatoes for the best results. To obtain the required level of crispiness, add extra oil as needed.
- For the best outcomes, keep an eye on the food while it cooks and take it out when the required level of brownness has been reached. In order to keep track of the interior temperatures of meat and fish, we advise utilising an instant-read thermometer.
- To achieve the greatest results, take food out of the air fryer as soon as the cooking process is finished.

Cleaning And Maintenance of the Dual Zone Air Fryer

Proper cleaning and maintenance of the Dual Zone Air Fryer is important to ensure optimal performance and a long lifespan for your air fryer.

1. First and foremost, it is important to clean the air fryer basket and crisper plate after each use. Unplug and let the air fryer cool before attempting to clean it. Simply remove the basket and crisper plate from the air fryer and wash them with warm, soapy water and a soft sponge or cloth to clean the basket and pan. Do not use harsh cleaning chemicals or scrubbing pads as these can damage the non-stick coating on the basket and pan.

2. Next, wipe down the inside and outside of your Dual Zone Air Fryer using a damp cloth to remove any splatters. Do not use harsh cleaners or scrubbers on the exterior of the air fryer as they can damage the finish.

3. Let all parts dried naturally after cleaning to prevent rusting. If any water is left on the metal parts, it will cause the parts to rust and this will damage the air fryer.

4. Once the basket and crisper plate are dry, place them back into the air fryer. Make sure the basket is positioned correctly in the air fryer so that it does not wobble or move around when in use. If the basket is not positioned correctly, it can cause the air fryer to work less efficiently.

5. To further maintain your air fryer, it is important to keep the air fryer unplugged when not in use and to store it in a cool, dry place. Do not store the air fryer in a humid or moist environment as this can lead to corrosion.

BREAKFAST RECIPES

Egg And Bacon Muffins

Preparation time: 5 minutes
Cooking time: 15 minutes
Serving: 1

Ingredients:
- 2 eggs
- 14ml green pesto
- 85g cheddar cheese, shredded
- 142g cooked bacon
- 1 onion, chopped
- Ground pepper & salt, to taste

Directions:
1. Beat the pesto, salt, pepper, and eggs in a bowl. Add the cheese and combine it well.
2. Pour the egg mixture into the cupcakes tin, then top with onion and cooked bacon.
3. Divide the cupcakes tin into two baskets and place it in the air fryer. Choose the "BAKE" for the first basket at 177°C and set the time to 15 minutes.
4. Choose the "MATCH COOK" for second basket and press the "START/PAUSE" to start cooking. Serve!

Nutrition: Calories: 134; Fat: 9.7g; Carbs: 1.4g; Protein: 10.1g

Breakfast Frittata

Preparation time: 10 minutes
Cooking time: 12 minutes
Servings: 4

Ingredients:
- 4 eggs
- 4 tbsp milk
- 35g cheddar cheese grated
- 50g feta crumbled
- 1 tomato, deseeded and chopped
- 15g spinach chopped
- 1 tbsp fresh herbs, chopped
- 2 spring onions chopped
- Salt & black pepper, to taste
- .50 tsp olive oil

Directions:
1. Beat the eggs with milk in your bowl, add the remaining ingredients, and stir well.
2. Grease two small-sized springform pans and lines them with parchment paper. Divide it into your pans and arrange them into your two air fryer baskets.
3. Place it in your air fryer. Choose the "AIR FRY" for the first basket at 180°C and set the time to 12 minutes.
4. Choose the "MATCH COOK" for second basket and press the "START/PAUSE" to start cooking. Serve!

Nutrition: Calories: 273; Fat: 22g; Carbs: 3g; Protein: 16g

Cheesy Onion Omelette

Preparation time: 10 minutes
Cooking time: 12 minutes
Servings: 2

Ingredients:
- 3 eggs
- 2ml soy sauce
- 1 onion, chopped
- 28g cheddar cheese, shredded
- pepper & salt, to taste

Directions:
1. Whisk the soy sauce, pepper, salt, and eggs into the bowl. Place the chopped onion over the mixture.
2. Divide the onion mixture into two baskets and place it in your air fryer. Choose the "AIR FRY" for the first basket at 180°C and set the time to 12 minutes.
3. Choose the "MATCH COOK" for second basket and press the "START/PAUSE" to start cooking. Serve!

Nutrition: Calories: 115; Fat: 9g; Carbs: 0g; Protein: 7g

Sausage Breakfast Casserole

Preparation time: 10 minutes
Cooking time: 20 minutes
Servings: 4

Ingredients:
- 455g hash browns
- 455g ground breakfast sausage
- 1 green capsicum diced
- 1 red capsicum, diced
- 1 yellow capsicum, diced
- 13g sweet onion, diced
- 4 eggs

Directions:
1. Arrange a parchment paper into your two-air fryer baskets, and divide the hash browns in each. Spread the sausage, onion, and peppers over the hash brown.
2. Place both baskets in your air fryer. Choose the "AIR FRY" for the first basket at 180°C and set the time to 10 minutes.
3. Choose the "MATCH COOK" for second basket and press the "START/PAUSE" to start cooking.
4. Beat the eggs in a bowl and pour over the air-fried veggies. Continue air frying for 10 minutes. Garnish with salt and black pepper before serving.

Nutrition: Calories: 267; Fat: 12g; Carbs: 39g; Protein: 3g

Mushroom And Squash Toast

Preparation time: 10 minutes
Cooking time: 10 minutes
Servings: 2

Ingredients:
- 14ml olive oil
- 1 red bell pepper, cut into strips
- 2 green onions, sliced
- 128g button or cremini mushrooms
- 1 yellow squash, sliced
- 29ml butter softened
- 4 slices of bread

- 64g soft cheese

Directions:
1. Divide vegetables into two baskets. Place both baskets in your air fryer. Choose "AIR FRY" for first basket at 177°C and set the time to 7 minutes.
2. Choose the "MATCH COOK" for second basket and press the "START/PAUSE" to start cooking. Set aside.
3. Spread the butter onto the slices of your bread and transfer it to the basket. Adjust the time to 3 minutes.
4. When done, remove and place cooked vegetables and cheese onto the toast. Serve.

Nutrition: Calories: 249; Fat: 7g; Carbs: 27g; Protein: 17g

Brussels Sprouts Potato Hash

Preparation time: 10 minutes
Cooking time: 10 minutes
Servings: 4
Ingredients:
- 455g Brussels sprouts, shredded
- 1 small to medium red onion
- 227g baby red potatoes, peeled, boiled, drained & diced
- 2 tbsp avocado oil
- .50 tsp salt
- .50 tsp black pepper

Directions:
1. Toss all the fixings in your large bowl. Divide this veggies hash mixture into both of the air fryer baskets.
2. Place both baskets in your air fryer. Choose the "AIR FRY" for the first basket at 190°C and set the time to 10 minutes.
3. Choose the "MATCH COOK" for second basket and press the "START/PAUSE" to start cooking. Serve!

Nutrition: Calories: 305; Fat: 25g; Carbs: 2g; Protein: 18g

Cinnamon Apple French Toast

Preparation time: 10 minutes
Cooking time: 10 minutes
Servings: 8
Ingredients:
- 1 egg, lightly beaten
- 4 bread slices
- 1 tbsp cinnamon
- 15ml milk
- 23ml maple syrup
- 45ml applesauce

Directions:
1. Whisk the egg, milk, cinnamon, applesauce, and maple syrup in your bowl.
2. Insert a crisper plate in the air fryer baskets. Dip each bread in the egg milk mixture and divide in your two air fryer baskets.
3. Choose the "AIR FRY" for the first basket at 180°C and set the time to 10 minutes.
4. Choose the "MATCH COOK" for second basket and press the "START/PAUSE" to start cooking. Serve!

Nutrition: Calories: 64; Fat: 1g; Carbs: 10g; Protein: 2g

Breakfast Stuffed Peppers

Preparation time: 10 minutes
Cooking time: 13 minutes
Servings: 4
Ingredients:
- 2 capsicums, halved, & seeds removed
- 4 eggs
- 1 tsp olive oil
- 1 pinch of each salt, pepper & sriracha flakes

Directions:
1. Place two capsicum halves in each air fryer basket. Add 1 egg into each capsicum halves and flavour it with the remaining fixings.
2. Place both baskets in your air fryer. Choose the "AIR FRY" for the first basket at 200°C and set the time to 13 minutes.
3. Choose the "MATCH COOK" for second basket and press the "START/PAUSE" to start cooking. Serve!

Nutrition: Calories: 237; Fat: 19g; Carbs: 7g; Protein: 12g

Pancake Doughnuts

Preparation time: 10 minutes
Cooking time: 9 minutes
Servings: 8

Ingredients:
- 2 eggs
- 50g sugar
- 125ml vegetable oil
- 240g pancake mix
- 1.50 tbsp cinnamon

Directions:
1. Combine the pancake mix, eggs, cinnamon, sugar, and oil in a bowl. Pour the doughnut mixture into the silicone doughnut moulds.
2. Insert a crisper plate in air fryer baskets. Place the doughnut moulds in both baskets.
3. Choose the "AIR FRY" for the first basket at 180°C and set the time to 9 minutes.
4. Choose the "MATCH COOK" for second basket and press the "START/PAUSE" to start cooking. Serve!

Nutrition: Calories: 163; Fat: 14g; Carbs: 7g; Protein: 1g

Morning Pumpkin Bread

Preparation time: 10 minutes
Cooking time: 45 minutes
Servings: 16 slices

Ingredients:
- 425g pumpkin pureed
- 3 eggs
- 236ml vegetable oil
- 320g sugar
- 384g flour
- 10g bicarb soda
- 5g salt
- 5g cinnamon
- 64g chocolate chips or cranberries (optional)

Directions:

1. Add the wet fixings into the bowl and blend it with a stand mixer. Add the dry fixings to another bowl and mix it well. Combine both dry and wet ingredients.
2. Fold into dried cranberries or chocolate chips. Divide the batter into two baskets and place it in the air fryer.
3. Choose the "AIR FRY" for the first basket at 165°C and set the time to 45 minutes.
4. Choose the "MATCH COOK" for second basket and press the "START/PAUSE" to start cooking. Serve!

Nutrition: Calories: 336; Fat: 15g; Carbs: 1g; Protein: 3g

Raspberry Nutella Toast Cups

Preparation time: 5 minutes
Cooking time: 8 minutes
Servings: 3

Ingredients:
- 6 slices of bread
- 10ml butter, melted
- 59ml Nutella
- 64g raspberry
- 28g powdered sugar

Directions:

1. Flatten the toast with a rolling pin, and brush it with butter on each side. Place each toast into the muffin tin and press it down.
2. Place the muffin tin into your two air fryer baskets. Choose the "BAKE" for the first basket at 160°C and set the time to 8 minutes.
3. Choose the "MATCH COOK" for second basket and press the "START/PAUSE" to start cooking.
4. When done, remove the muffins, add Nutella to the bread cup and top with raspberries. Sprinkle with powdered sugar before serving.

Nutrition: Calories: 196; Fat: 10g; Carbs: 24g; Protein: 2g

Breakfast Potatoes

Preparation time: 15 minutes
Cooking time: 20 minutes
Servings: 6

Ingredients:
- 3 potatoes, peeled and diced
- 1 onion yellow, diced
- 1 green pepper diced
- 2 tsp salt
- .50 tsp pepper
- 2 tbsp olive oil
- 1 cup shredded cheese

Directions:
1. Toss the potatoes with onion, green peppers, black pepper, salt and cheese in a bowl. Divide the potato mixture into the air fryer baskets.
2. Place both baskets in your air fryer. Choose the "AIR FRY" for the first basket at 200°C and set the time to 20 minutes.
3. Choose the "MATCH COOK" for second basket and press the "START/PAUSE" to start cooking. Serve!

Nutrition: Calories: 209; Fat: 7g; Carbs: 34g; Protein: 4g

Cheesy Egg Ramekins

Preparation time: 10 minutes
Cooking time: 16 minutes
Servings: 4

Ingredients:
- 4 large eggs
- 57g smoked gouda, shredded
- Everything bagel seasoning, to taste
- Salt & pepper to taste

Directions:
1. Add one egg among your 4 ramekins. Flavour it with the remaining fixings. Place 2 ramekins in each air fryer basket.
2. Place both baskets in your air fryer. Choose the "AIR FRY" for the first basket at 177°C and set the time to 16 minutes.
3. Choose the "MATCH COOK" for second basket and press the "START/PAUSE" to start cooking. Serve!

Nutrition: Calories: 190; Fat: 18g; Carbs: 0g; Protein: 7g

Turkey Ham Muffins

Preparation time: 10 minutes
Cooking time: 10 minutes
Servings: 16 muffins

Ingredients:
- 1 egg
- 340g all-purpose flour
- 85g turkey ham, chopped
- 2 tbsp mixed herbs, chopped
- 235g cheddar cheese, shredded
- 1 onion, chopped
- 2 tsp baking powder
- 2 tbsp butter, melted
- 237ml milk
- salt & pepper to taste

Directions:
1. Mix the baking powder plus flour in your large bowl. Add the egg, butter, and milk, then mix until well combined.
2. Add the herbs, cheese, onion, and turkey ham, then mix well. Pour the batter into the silicone muffin moulds and divide it into both baskets.
3. Place both baskets in your air fryer. Choose the "AIR FRY" for the first basket at 180°C and set the time to 10 minutes.
4. Choose the "MATCH COOK" for second basket and press the "START/PAUSE" to start cooking. Serve!

Nutrition: Calories: 140; Fat: 4g; Carbs: 18g; Protein: 5g

Sweet Potato Hash

Preparation time: 10 minutes
Cooking time: 15 minutes
Servings: 4

Ingredients:
- 3 sweet potatoes, peel & cut into 1.27-cm pieces
- .50 tsp cinnamon
- 2 tbsp olive oil
- 1 bell pepper, cut into 1.27-cm pieces
- .50 tsp dried thyme
- .50 tsp nutmeg
- 1 medium onion, cut into 1.27-cm pieces
- Salt & pepper to taste

Directions:
1. Toss all the fixings in your bowl. Divide the potato mixture into the two air fryer baskets.
2. Place both baskets in your air fryer. Choose the "AIR FRY" for the first basket at 180°C and set the time to 15 minutes.
3. Choose the "MATCH COOK" for second basket, and press the "START/PAUSE" to start cooking. Serve!

Nutrition: Calories: 167; Fat: 7g; Carbs: 24g; Protein: 2g

POULTRY RECIPES

Chicken Leg Barbecue

Preparation time: 10 minutes
Cooking time: 40 minutes
Servings: 2

Ingredients:
- 2 chicken leg quarters
- 59ml barbecue sauce
- salt & pepper, to taste

Directions:
1. Brush the chicken legs with olive oil, and season them with pepper and salt. Divide the chicken legs into the two air fryer baskets.
2. Place both baskets in your air fryer. Choose the "AIR FRY" for the first basket at 195°C and set the time to 35 minutes.
3. Choose the "MATCH COOK" for second basket, and press the "START/PAUSE" to start cooking. Baste it with the sauce halfway cooking and let it rest before serving.

Nutrition: Calories: 168; Fat: 8g; Carbs: 5g; Protein: 20g

Pistachio Crusted Chicken

Preparation time: 10 minutes
Cooking time: 18 minutes
Servings: 2

Ingredients:
- 170g skinless chicken breast
- 2g salt
- 1g pepper
- 29ml mayonnaise
- 64g pistachios, roasted & salted
- 15ml olive oil

Directions:
1. Season the chicken breast with pepper and salt. Top it with mayonnaise over chicken breast.
2. Sprinkle the pistachios on each piece of chicken breast. Divide the chicken breast mixture into the two air fryer baskets.
3. Place both baskets in your air fryer. Choose the "AIR FRY" for the first basket at 195°C and set the time to 18 minutes.
4. Choose the "MATCH COOK" for second basket, and press the "START/PAUSE" to start cooking. Serve!

Nutrition: Calories: 332; Fat: 31g; Carbs: 9g; Protein: 58g

Popcorn Chicken

Preparation time: 15 minutes
Cooking time: 10 minutes
Servings: 6

Ingredients:
- 454g chicken breasts, boneless, cut into bite-size pieces
- 128g panko bread crumbs
- 128g flour
- 5g chilli flakes
- 10g oregano
- 10g onion powder
- 10g garlic powder
- 10g pepper
- 10g salt
- 1 egg

Directions:
1. Rinse the chicken and pat it dry with a paper towel—season with oregano, garlic powder, onion powder, chilli flakes, black pepper, and salt. Let it rest for 10 minutes.
2. Dip the chicken pieces into the flour and then in the egg. Then, dredge in the breadcrumbs. Divide the coated chicken cutlets into two air fryer baskets.

3. Place both baskets in your air fryer. Choose the "AIR FRY" for the first basket at 177°C and set the time to 10 minutes.
4. Choose the "MATCH COOK" for second basket, and press the "START/PAUSE" to start cooking. Serve!

Nutrition: Calories: 253; Fat: 4g; Carbs: 31g; Protein: 22g

Buffalo Chicken Calzones

Preparation time: 10 minutes
Cooking time: 10 minutes
Servings: 4

Ingredients:
- 171g cooked chicken, shredded
- 59ml buffalo wing sauce
- 171g mozzarella cheese, shredded
- 32g blue cheese crumbles
- 1 tube pizza crust, refrigerated

Directions:
1. Spread a sheet of pizza dough onto the clean work surface, and slice it into squares. Cut each square into a circle with a pizza cutter.
2. Combine the blue cheese crumbles, buffalo sauce, and chicken into the bowl—top one-half of each circle of dough with shredded cheese and chicken.
3. Fold it over the cheese and meat, then seal it. Spray each calzone with olive oil. Divide the calzones into two baskets.
4. Place both baskets in your air fryer. Choose the "AIR FRY" for the first basket at 162°C and set the time to 10 minutes.
5. Choose the "MATCH COOK" for second basket, and press the "START/PAUSE" to start cooking. Serve!

Nutrition: Calories: 580; Fat: 22g; Carbs: 55g; Protein: 29g

Chicken Burger

Preparation time: 10 minutes
Cooking time: 18 minutes
Servings: 4

Ingredients:
- 454g ground chicken
- 64g seasoned bread crumbs
- 32g parmesan cheese, grated
- 1 egg, beaten
- 14g garlic, minced
- 5ml Worcestershire sauce

Directions:
1. Mix the Worcestershire sauce, garlic, egg, parmesan cheese, breadcrumbs, and ground chicken into the bowl. Make patties from the mixture. Place it into the refrigerator for 15 minutes to 1 hour.
2. Divide chicken patties into two baskets. Place both baskets in your air fryer. Choose the "AIR FRY" for the first basket at 190°C and set the time to 18 minutes.
3. Choose the "MATCH COOK" for second basket, and press the "START/PAUSE" to start cooking. Serve!

Nutrition: Calories: 318; Fat: 16g; Carbs: 12g; Protein: 32g

Chicken Sausage Pizza

Preparation time: 10 minutes
Cooking time: 9 minutes
Servings: 6

Ingredients:
- 1 piece of naan bread
- 59ml barbeque sauce
- 32g mozzarella cheese
- 32g gouda cheese
- half of the red onion, thinly sliced
- half of the chicken sausage

Directions:
1. Place the BBQ sauce over the naan bread and top with red onion, Gouda cheese, and mozzarella cheese. Place the chicken sausage on top and spray with cooking spray.
2. Divide it into two baskets. Place both baskets in your air fryer. Choose the "AIR FRY" for the first basket at 200°C and set the time to 9 minutes.
3. Choose the "MATCH COOK" for second basket, and press the "START/PAUSE" to start cooking. Serve!

Nutrition: Calories: 643; Fat: 23g; Carbs: 76g; Protein: 31g

Chicken Meatballs

Preparation time: 10 minutes
Cooking time: 15 minutes
Servings: 4
Ingredients:
- 454g minced chicken breast
- 128g breadcrumbs
- 1 egg
- 14g Italian seasoning
- 5g ground black pepper
- 64g parmesan cheese
- 177ml marinara sauce
- 64g mozzarella cheese, shredded

Directions:
1. Combine the seasoning, egg, parmesan cheese, chicken, and breadcrumbs in the mixing bowl. Shape the mixture into meatballs.
4. Divide meatballs into two baskets. Place both baskets in your air fryer. Choose the "AIR FRY" for the first basket at 176°C and set the time to 15 minutes.
2. Choose the "MATCH COOK" for second basket, and press the "START/PAUSE" to start cooking.
3. Open the lid, and top with marinara sauce and mozzarella cheese. Serve!

Nutrition: Calories: 391; Fat: 18g; Carbs: 24g; Protein: 33g

Lemon Chicken Thighs

Preparation time: 10 minutes
Cooking time: 22 minutes
Servings: 4

Ingredients:
- 55g butter, softened
- 3 garlic cloves, minced
- 2 tsp minced fresh rosemary
- 1 tsp minced fresh thyme
- 1 tsp grated lemon zest
- 1 tbsp lemon juice
- 4 (about 675 g) bone-in chicken thighs
- salt & pepper to taste

Directions:
1. Mix the butter, thyme, rosemary, garlic, lemon zest, and juice in your bowl.
2. Under the skin of each chicken thigh, spread 1 tsp butter mixture. Apply the remaining butter to each thigh's skin—season to taste with salt and pepper.
3. Install a crisper plate in both drawers. Place half the chicken tenders in the zone 1 basket and half in zone 2's, then insert the basket into the air fryer.
4. Choose the "AIR FRY" for the first basket at 200°C and set the time to 22 minutes.
5. Choose the "MATCH COOK" for second basket, and press the "START/PAUSE" to start cooking.
6. Halfway through the cooking time, press START/ PAUSE to pause the air fryer. Flip the chicken, and press START/STOP to resume cooking. Serve.

Nutrition: Calories: 329; Fat: 26g; Carbs: 1g; Protein: 23g

Cornish Hen with Asparagus

Preparation time: 15 minutes
Cooking time: 53 minutes
Servings: 2

Ingredients:
- 10 spears asparagus
- salt & black pepper, to taste
- 1 Cornish hen
- 1 tsp paprika
- coconut spray for greasing

Directions:
1. Wash and pat dry the asparagus and coat it with coconut oil spray. Sprinkle it with salt and place them in the zone 1 basket.
2. Rub the Cornish hen with salt, black pepper, and paprika. Oil spray the Cornish hen and place it in the second air fryer basket.
3. Place both baskets in your air fryer. Choose the "AIR FRY" for the first basket at 175°C and set the time to 8 minutes.
4. For zone 2, choose the "ROAST" for the first basket at 175°C and set the time to 45 minutes.
5. Press the "START/PAUSE" to start cooking. Serve the chicken with the vegetables.

Nutrition: Calories: 192; Fat: 4g; Carbs: 10g; Protein: 30g

Cornish Hen with Baked Potatoes

Preparation time: 15 minutes
Cooking time: 45 minutes
Servings: 2

Ingredients:
- 1 large potato, pierced
- 1 tbsp avocado oil
- 680g Cornish hen, whole & skinless
- 2-3 tsp dry rub poultry seasoning
- Salt, to taste

Directions:
1. Rub the potato with avocado oil and salt. Place the potato in the zone 1 basket.
2. Coat the Cornish hen thoroughly with poultry seasoning and salt. Place the hen in the zone 2 basket.
3. Place both baskets in your air fryer. Choose the "AIR FRY" for the first basket at 175°C and set the time to 45 minutes.
4. Choose the "MATCH COOK" for second basket, and press the "START/PAUSE" to start cooking. Serve!

Nutrition: Calories: 612; Fat: 14g; Carbs: 33g; Protein: 83g

Air Fried Turkey Breast

Preparation time: 10 minutes
Cooking time: 46 minutes
Servings: 4

Ingredients:
- 908g turkey breast, on the bone with skin
- 15ml olive oil
- 1 tsp salt
- .25 tbsp dry poultry seasoning

Directions:
1. Rub turkey breast with 7.5ml oil. Season both sides with turkey seasoning and salt, then brush the remaining oil over the turkey's skin.
2. Divide the turkey in half and place each half into the two air fryer baskets. Place both baskets in your air fryer. Choose the "AIR FRY" for the first basket at 200°C and set the time to 46 minutes.
3. Choose the "MATCH COOK" for second basket, and press the "START/PAUSE" to start cooking.
4. Flip the turkey once cooked halfway through, and resume cooking. Slice and serve warm.

Nutrition: Calories: 502; Fat: 25g; Carbs: 1g; Protein: 64g

Roasted Turkey with Cauliflower

Preparation time: 10 minutes
Cooking time: 52-53 minutes
Servings: 4

Ingredients:
- 908g turkey thighs
- 454g cauliflower, broken into small florets
- 14ml butter
- 2g smoked paprika
- 2g dried marjoram
- 1g dried dill
- salt & ground black pepper, to taste
- 43g grated cheese
- 5g minced garlic

Directions:
1. Rub the butter all over the turkey thighs and sprinkle with black pepper, salt, dill, marjoram, and smoked paprika.
2. Toss the cauliflower florets with garlic, salt, and cheese.
3. Place the coated turkey thighs in the zone 1 basket. Place the crisper plate into the zone 2 basket, and add the cauliflower florets mixture into the zone 2 basket.

4. Choose the "ROAST" for the first basket at 185°C and set the time to 40 minutes.
5. For zone 2, choose the "AIR FRY" at 200°C and set the time to 12 to 13 minutes of cooking time. Press the "START/PAUSE" to start cooking. Serve!

Nutrition: Calories: 315; Fat: 7g; Carbs: 7g; Protein: 3g

Turkey Burger Patties

Preparation time: 10 minutes
Cooking time: 14 minutes
Servings: 4

Ingredients:
- 1 egg white
- 453g minced turkey
- 30ml Worcestershire sauce
- .50 tsp dried basil
- .50 tsp dried oregano
- salt & pepper to taste

Directions:
1. Mix the minced turkey with the remaining ingredients in a bowl until well combined.
2. Make patties from the turkey mixture and place them in both baskets. Insert a crisper plate in the air fryer baskets.
3. Choose the "AIR FRY" for the first basket at 182°C and set the time to 14 minutes.
4. Choose the "MATCH COOK" for second basket, and press the "START/PAUSE" to start cooking. Serve!

Nutrition: Calories: 234; Fat: 12g; Carbs: 2g; Protein: 32g

Tarragon Turkey with Baby Potatoes

Preparation time: 10 minutes
Cooking time: 45 minutes
Servings: 6

Ingredients:
- 908g turkey tenderloins
- 454g baby potatoes, rubbed
- 10ml olive oil
- salt & ground black pepper, to taste
- 4g smoked paprika
- 29ml dry white wine
- 14g fresh tarragon leaves, chopped

Directions:
1. Brush the turkey tenderloin with olive oil. Sprinkle it with pepper, salt, and paprika. Add the tarragon and white wine. Place the turkey tenderloin into the Zone 1 basket.
2. Place the crisper plate into the Zone 2 basket, and add the baby potatoes into the basket.
3. Choose the "ROAST" for the first basket at 176°C and set the time to 30 minutes.
4. For zone 2, choose the "AIR FRY" at 200°C and set the time to 15 minutes. Press the "START/PAUSE" to start cooking.
5. Transfer chicken tenderloin into the bowl and serve with fried baby potatoes.

Nutrition: Calories: 317; Fat: 7g; Carbs: 14g; Protein: 45g

Turkey Sausage with Brussels

Preparation time: 10 minutes
Cooking time: 25 minutes
Servings: 2

Ingredients:
- 454g turkey sausages
- 227g brussels sprouts, trimmed and halved
- 5ml olive oil
- salt & ground black pepper, to taste
- 2g cayenne pepper
- 2g onion granules
- 1g dried dill weed

Directions:
1. Place turkey sausages into the Zone 1 basket.
2. Combine the Brussels sprouts, olive oil, dill weed onion granules, cayenne pepper, ground black pepper, and salt in your large bowl.
3. Place the crisper plate into the Zone 2 basket, and add the coated Brussels sprouts.
4. Choose the "AIR FRY" for the first basket at 193°C and set the time to 15 minutes.
5. For zone 2, choose the " ROAST " at 187°C and set the time to 10 minutes. Press the "START/PAUSE" to start cooking.
6. Serve the chicken sausages with the roasted Brussels sprouts.

Nutrition: Calories: 601; Fat: 40g; Carbs: 16g; Protein: 39g

BEEF, PORK AND LAMB RECIPES

Beef Meatloaf

Preparation time: 10 minutes
Cooking time: 25 minutes
Servings: 4

Ingredients:
- 454g lean minced beef
- 1 egg, beaten
- 42g dry bread crumbs
- 1 onion, chopped
- 14g fresh thyme, chopped
- 5g salt
- ground black pepper, to taste
- 2 mushrooms, thickly sliced
- 14ml olive oil

Directions:
1. Mix the pepper, thyme, salt, onion, egg, breadcrumbs, and minced beef in the bowl. Knead to combine it well.
2. Let it smooth with your hand, add the mushrooms, and coat it with olive oil. Knead it again. Divide the mixture into the air fryer baskets.
5. Place both baskets in your air fryer. Choose the "AIR FRY" for the first basket at 200°C and set the time to 25 minutes.
3. Choose the "MATCH COOK" for second basket, and press the "START/PAUSE" to start cooking. Serve!

Nutrition: Calories: 297; Fat: 18g; Carbs: 5g; Protein: 24g

Garlic Sirloin Steak

Preparation time: 10 minutes
Cooking time: 10 minutes
Servings: 4

Ingredients:
- 4 sirloin steak
- 30ml olive oil
- 28g steak sauce
- .50 tsp ground coriander
- 1 tsp garlic, minced
- 1 tbsp thyme, chopped
- salt & pepper to taste

Directions:
1. Mix all the fixings in your bowl, and marinate for 2 hours.
2. Insert a crisper plate in your air fryer baskets. Divide the marinated steaks into both baskets.
3. Choose the "AIR FRY" for the first basket at 182°C and set the time to 10 minutes.
4. Choose the "MATCH COOK" for second basket, and press the "START/PAUSE" to start cooking. Serve!

Nutrition: Calories: 348; Fat: 18g; Carbs: 0g; Protein: 0g

Beef Kofta Kebab

Preparation time: 10 minutes
Cooking time: 18 minutes
Servings: 4

Ingredients:
- 455g minced beef
- 13g white onion, grated
- 15g parsley, chopped
- 1 tbsp mint, chopped
- 2 cloves garlic, minced
- 1 tsp salt
- .50 tsp cumin
- 1 tsp oregano
- .50 tsp garlic salt
- 1 egg

Directions:
1. Mix the minced beef with onion, parsley, mint, garlic, cumin, oregano, garlic salt and egg in a bowl. Make the kebabs out of this mixture.
5. Divide it into two air fryer baskets. Place both basket in your air fryer. Choose the "AIR FRY" for the first basket at 190°C and set the time to 18 minutes.
2. Choose the "MATCH COOK" for second basket, and press the "START/PAUSE" to start cooking. Serve!

Nutrition: Calories: 316; Fat: 12g; Carbs: 12g; Protein: 25g

Marinated Steak & Mushrooms

Preparation time: 10 minutes + marinating time
Cooking time: 10 minutes
Servings: 4

Ingredients:
- 450g rib-eye steak, cut into 1.27-cm pieces
- 2 tsp dark soy sauce
- 2 tsp light soy sauce
- 15ml lime juice
- 15ml rice wine
- 15ml oyster sauce
- 1 tbsp garlic, chopped
- 8 mushrooms, sliced
- 2 tbsp ginger, grated
- 1 tsp cornflour
- .25 tsp pepper

Directions:
1. Add all the fixings to a zip-lock bag. Seal it and place it in your refrigerator for 2 hours.
2. Insert a crisper plate in the air fryer baskets. Divide the marinated steaks and mushrooms into both air fryer baskets.
3. Choose the "AIR FRY" for the first basket at 193°C and set the time to 10 minutes.
4. Choose the "MATCH COOK" for second basket, and press the "START/PAUSE" to start cooking. Stir it halfway through. Serve!

Nutrition: Calories: 341; Fat: 25g; Carbs: 6g; Protein: 21g

Cheesesteak Taquitos

Preparation time: 15 minutes
Cooking time: 12 minutes
Servings: 8

Ingredients:
- 136g beef steak strips
- 1 pack of soft corn tortillas
- 2 green peppers, sliced
- 1 white onion, chopped
- 1 pack of dry Italian dressing mix
- 10 slices of Cheddar cheese
- Cooking spray or olive oil

Directions:
1. Mix the beef with oil, peppers, onion, and Italian dressing in a bowl. Divide the strips into two air fryer baskets.
6. Place both baskets in your air fryer. Choose the "AIR FRY" for the first basket at 190°C and set the time to 12 minutes.
2. Choose the "MATCH COOK" for second basket, and press the "START/PAUSE" to start cooking. Flip the strips once cooked halfway through.
3. Divide the beef strips in the tortillas and top the beef with a cheese slice. Roll the tortillas and serve.

Nutrition: Calories: 410; Fat: 17g; Carbs: 21g; Protein: 38g

Pork Chop with Mushrooms

Preparation time: 10 minutes
Cooking time: 18 minutes
Servings: 4

Ingredients:
- 454g pork belly or pork chops, rinsed, pat dry & cut into cubes
- 226g mushrooms, cleaned, washed & halved
- 30ml butter, melted
- 5ml Worcestershire sauce or soy sauce
- 2g garlic powder
- salt & black pepper, to taste

Directions:
1. Mix the pork chops with the mushrooms in your large bowl. Coat it with butter, then flavour it with pepper, salt, garlic powder, and Worcestershire sauce.
2. Divide the pork and mushroom mixture into two air fryer baskets.
7. Place both baskets in your air fryer. Choose the "AIR FRY" for the first basket at 200°C and set the time to 18 minutes.
3. Choose the "MATCH COOK" for second basket, and press the "START/PAUSE" to start cooking. Serve!

Nutrition: Calories: 241; Fat: 14g; Carbs: 2g; Protein: 26g

Courgette Pork Skewers

Preparation time: 15 minutes + marinating time
Cooking time: 23 minutes
Servings: 4

Ingredients:
- 1 large courgette, cut 2.5-cm pieces
- 450g boneless pork belly, cut into cubes
- 1 yellow onion, diced in squares
- 300g grape tomatoes
- 1 garlic clove minced
- 1 lemon, juice only
- 60ml olive oil
- 2 tbsp balsamic vinegar
- 1 tsp oregano
- olive oil spray

Directions:
1. Mix the balsamic vinegar, garlic, oregano lemon juice, and 60ml of olive oil in a large bowl. Add the diced pork pieces and mix well to coat.
2. Leave the seasoned pork to marinate for 60 minutes in the refrigerator.
3. Take suitable wooden skewers for your air fryer's drawer, and thread the marinated pork and vegetables alternately on each skewer.
4. Place half of the skewers in each crisper plate and spray them with cooking oil.
5. Choose the "AIR FRY" for the first basket at 200°C and set the time to 23 minutes.
6. Choose the "MATCH COOK" for second basket, and press the "START/PAUSE" to start cooking. Flip the skewers once cooked halfway through, and resume cooking. Serve!

Nutrition: Calories: 459; Fat: 17g; Carbs: 2g; Protein: 49g

Pork Lettuce Wraps

Preparation time: 10 minutes + marinating time
Cooking time: 10 minutes
Servings: 4

Ingredients:
- 454g pork tenderloin, cut into 1.27-cm slices
- 59ml chilli sauce
- 59ml soy sauce, low-sodium
- 3 spring onions, chopped
- 256g cooked brown rice
- 12 butter lettuce leaves
- 128g English cucumber, thinly sliced
- 128g carrots, shredded
- 7g sesame seeds
- 2 onions, sliced

Directions:
1. Mix the pork pieces, soy sauce and chilli sauce into a bowl. Cover, and marinate for 2 hours in your fridge.
8. Divide the pork pieces into two air fryer baskets. Choose the "AIR FRY" for the first basket at 200°C and set the time to 10 minutes.
2. Choose the "MATCH COOK" for second basket, and press the "START/PAUSE" to start cooking. Serve!

Nutrition: Calories: 607; Fat: 44g; Carbs: 19g; Protein: 34g

Pork Chops Parmigiana

Preparation time: 10 minutes
Cooking time: 10-14 minutes
Servings: 3

Ingredients:
- 170g pork chops, rinsed and patted dry
- garlic powder, smoked paprika, salt & black pepper to taste
- 54g breadcrumbs
- 50g parmesan cheese, grated
- 28g parsley, chopped
- 1 egg
- 56g mozzarella cheese
- 240ml marinara sauce

Directions:
1. Flavour the pork chops with garlic powder, paprika, pepper, and salt.
2. Combine the chopped parsley, parmesan cheese, and breadcrumbs in a bowl. Beat the egg to another bowl.
3. Dip each chop in the egg, then coat it in the breadcrumb mixture.
9. Divide it into two air fryer baskets. Place both baskets in your air fryer. Choose the "AIR FRY" for the first basket at 194°C and set the time to 12 minutes.
4. Choose the "MATCH COOK" for second basket, and press the "START/PAUSE" to start cooking.
5. Open, sprinkle it with cheese and cook for 2 minutes more. Serve with marinara sauce.

Nutrition: Calories: 495; Fat: 22g; Carbs: 18g; Protein: 53g

Sausage Stuffed Courgette Boats

Preparation time: 15 minutes
Cooking time: 10 minutes
Servings: 4

Ingredients:
- 2 courgettes, halved & cored
- 227g uncooked sausage meat
- 32g breadcrumbs
- 57g cheese, grated
- 28g parsley, chopped

Directions:
1. Place courgettes onto the clean work surface and spray with olive oil.
2. Flip the courgettes, stuff them with sausage meat, and then top them with cheese and breadcrumbs.
3. Divide the stuffed courgettes into two air fryer baskets. Place both baskets in your air fryer.
4. Choose the "AIR FRY" for the first basket at 180°C and set the time to 14 minutes.
5. Choose the "MATCH COOK" for second basket, and press the "START/PAUSE" to start cooking. Garnish with parsley leaves. Serve!

Nutrition: Calories: 285; Fat: 21g; Carbs: 9g; Protein: 16g

Pork Schnitzel

Nutrition: Calories: 461; Fat: 21g; Carbs: 25g; Protein: 42g

Preparation time: 10 minutes
Cooking time: 14 minutes
Servings: 4

Ingredients:
- 4 pork chops, boneless, cut or pounded to a .85-cm thickness
- 1g thyme
- .50g garlic salt
- 1g fajita seasoning
- 1g dried sage
- 1g fresh rosemary, minced
- 1 egg
- 64g all-purpose flour
- salt & pepper, to taste
- 85g panko breadcrumbs

Directions:
1. Mix the breadcrumbs and spices into a bowl. Add the pepper and salt. Add the egg to a second bowl. Add the flour to the third bowl.
2. Coat the chop in the flour and then dip it in the egg wash. Then, dredge into the panko mixture.
3. Divide the pork chops into the two air fryer baskets.
4. Place both baskets in your air fryer. Choose the "AIR FRY" for the first basket at 198°C and set the time to 14 minutes.
5. Choose the "MATCH COOK" for second basket, and press the "START/PAUSE" to start cooking. Serve!

Mint Glazed Leg of Lamb

Preparation time: 10 minutes
Cooking time: 1 hour & 20 minutes
Servings: 4

Ingredients:
For the Lamb:
- 1.3kg boneless leg of lamb, patted dry
- 3 cloves of garlic
- 30ml olive oil
- 2g sea salt
- 1g cracked pepper

For the Mint glaze:
- 43g mint leaves, chopped
- 28g brown sugar
- 36ml malt vinegar
- 30ml boiled water
- 5g salt

Directions:
1. Cut slits into the lamb's skin with a sharp knife. Cut garlic into slivers and insert one piece into each slice.
2. Drizzle it with olive oil and flavour it with pepper and salt. Divide the lamb mixture into two baskets.
3. Place both baskets in your air fryer. Choose the "AIR FRY" for the first basket at 194°C and set the time to 20 minutes.
4. Choose the "MATCH COOK" for second basket, and press the "START/PAUSE" to start cooking.
5. Meanwhile, mix the salt, brown sugar, and boiled water in a bowl. Add the mint and malt vinegar, then mix it well. Keep it aside.
6. Open the air fryer's lid, baste the lamb with a mint glaze and cook for 20 minutes. Baste the lamb often until you get desired consistency. Let it rest before serving.

Nutrition: Calories: 406; Fat: 19g; Carbs: 9g; Protein: 46g

Greek Lamb Burgers

Preparation time: 10 minutes
Cooking time: 20 minutes
Servings: 4

Ingredients:
- 681g minced lamb
- 5g oregano
- 43g feta cheese, crumbled
- 2g salt & pepper
- 4 buns, halved
- half a head of lettuce
- 1 tomato
- 236ml Greek yoghurt

Directions:
1. Combine the pepper, feta cheese, oregano, and minced lamb in a bowl—season with pepper and salt. Make the patties out of this mixture. Divide the patties into two air fryer baskets.
2. Place both baskets in your air fryer. Choose the "AIR FRY" for the first basket at 190°C and set the time to 10 minutes.
3. Choose the "MATCH COOK" for second basket, and press the "START/PAUSE" to start cooking. Let it rest for 5 minutes.
4. Arrange the patties with the tomato slices, lettuce leaves, and yoghurt between buns, then serve.

Nutrition: Calories: 790; Fat: 21g; Carbs: 40g; Protein: 38g

Mustard Lamb Chops

Preparation time: 15 minutes + marinating time
Cooking time: 32 minutes
Servings: 4

Ingredients:
- 4 pieces of lamb chops
- 1 tsp Dijon mustard
- 1 tsp olive oil
- .50 tsp soy sauce
- .50 tsp garlic, minced
- .50 tsp cumin powder
- .50 tsp cayenne pepper
- .50 tsp Italian spice blend
- .125 tsp salt

Directions:
1. Mix the Dijon mustard, soy sauce, olive oil, garlic, cumin powder, cayenne pepper, Italian spice blend, and salt in a medium bowl.
2. Place the lamb chops into a Ziploc bag and pour in the marinade. Close, and knead the bag until the chops are well coated.
3. Keep them in the fridge and marinate for at least 30 minutes or overnight.
4. Place 2 chops in each crisper plate and spray them with cooking oil. Return the crisper plate to the air fryer.
5. Choose the "ROAST" for the first basket at 177°C and set the time to 27 minutes.
6. Choose the "MATCH COOK" for second basket, and press the "START/PAUSE" to start cooking. Flip the chops once cooked halfway through, and resume cooking.

7. Switch the "ROAST" mode to "MAX CRISP" mode and cook for 5 minutes. Serve warm.

Nutrition: Calories: 264; Fat: 17g; Carbs: 1g; Protein: 27g

Nutrition: Calories: 396; Fat: 23g; Carbs: 0g; Protein: 45g

Lemony Lamb Chops

Preparation time: 10 minutes
Cooking time: 10 minutes
Servings: 4

Ingredients:
- 700g lamb chops
- .50 tsp oregano
- 3 tbsp parsley, minced
- .50 tsp black pepper
- 3 cloves minced garlic
- 2 tbsp lemon juice
- 2 tbsp olive oil
- Salt to taste

Directions:
1. Pat dry the chops and mix with the remaining ingredients. Divide these chops into the two air fryer baskets.
2. Place both baskets in your air fryer. Choose the "AIR FRY" for the first basket at 200°C and set the time to 10 minutes.
3. Choose the "MATCH COOK" for second basket, and press the "START/PAUSE" to start cooking. Flip the pork chops once cooked halfway through. Serve!

FISH AND SEAFOOD RECIPES

Salmon Cakes

Preparation time: 10 minutes
Cooking time: 10 minutes
Servings: 4

Ingredients:
- 454g salmon, deboned
- 2 eggs
- 14ml mayonnaise
- half of the red bell pepper
- 64g breadcrumbs
- 2g garlic powder
- 2g black pepper
- 1g salt
- 28g parsley, chopped
- olive oil spray

Directions:
1. Combine the seasonings, egg, salmon, and breadcrumbs in the bowl. Make the patties out of this mixture. Divide the patties into two air fryer baskets.
2. Place both baskets in your air fryer. Choose the "AIR FRY" for the first basket at 198°C and set the time to 10 minutes.
3. Choose the "MATCH COOK" for second basket, and press the "START/PAUSE" to start cooking. Serve!

Nutrition: Calories: 273; Fat: 13g; Carbs: 11g; Protein: 26g

Chili Lime Tilapia

Preparation time: 15 minutes
Cooking time: 10 minutes
Servings: 4

Ingredients:
- 340g tilapia fillets
- 2 tsp chilli powder
- 1 tsp cumin
- 1 tsp garlic powder
- .50 tsp oregano
- .50 tsp sea salt
- .25 tsp black pepper
- Lime zest from 1 lime
- Juice half of lime

Directions:
1. Mix the chilli powder and other spices with lime juice and zest in a bowl. Rub this spice mixture over the tilapia fillets.
2. Place two fillets in each air basket. Place both baskets in your air fryer. Choose the "AIR FRY" for the first basket at 200°C and set the time to 10 minutes.
3. Choose the "MATCH COOK" for second basket, and press the "START/PAUSE" to start cooking. Flip the tilapia fillets once cooked halfway through. Serve!

Nutrition: Calories: 275; Fat: 1g; Carbs: 31g; Protein: 29g

Blackened Cod Fish

Preparation time: 15 minutes
Cooking time: 17 minutes
Servings: 2

Ingredients:
- 400g black cod, cut into 2 steaks
- 14g garlic clove, minced
- 5g soy sauce
- 2g granulated sugar
- 2g salt
- 2g ground black pepper
- coriander and jalapeno for garnish

Directions:
1. Combine the pepper, salt, sugar, soy sauce, and garlic in the zip-lock bag. Add the cod steaks, knead the bag and marinate the cod for 30 minutes.
2. Divide the mixture into two air fryer baskets. Place both baskets in your air fryer. Choose the "AIR FRY" for the first basket at 176°C and set the time to 17 minutes.
3. Choose the "MATCH COOK" for second basket, and press the "START/PAUSE" to start cooking. Serve!

Nutrition: Calories: 194; Fat: 2g; Carbs: 8g; Protein: 36g

Marinated Tuna Steaks

Preparation time: 10 minutes
Cooking time: 5 minutes
Servings: 2

Ingredients:
- 170g tuna steaks, boneless, & skinless
- 59ml soy sauce
- 10ml honey
- 5g ginger, grated
- 5ml sesame oil
- 2ml rice vinegar

Directions:
1. Mix all the fixings in your bowl, and marinate the tuna in the refrigerator for 20 to 30 minutes.
2. Divide the mixture into the two air fryer baskets. Place both baskets in your air fryer. Choose the "AIR FRY" for the first basket at 193°C and set the time to 5 minutes.
3. Choose the "MATCH COOK" for second basket, and press the "START/PAUSE" to start cooking. Serve.

Nutrition: Calories: 422; Fat: 23g; Carbs: 8g; Protein: 44g

Brown Sugar Garlic Salmon

Preparation time: 15 minutes
Cooking time: 10 minutes
Servings: 4

Ingredients:
- 455g salmon
- Salt & black pepper, to taste
- 2 tbsp brown sugar
- 1 tsp chilli powder
- .50 tsp paprika
- 1 tsp Italian seasoning
- 1 tsp garlic powder

Directions:
1. Mix the brown sugar with garlic powder, Italian seasoning, paprika, and chilli powder in a bowl. Rub this

mixture over the salmon, then season it with black pepper and salt.
2. Divide the salmon into two air fryer baskets. Place both baskets in your air fryer. Choose the "AIR FRY" for the first basket at 200°C and set the time to 10 minutes.
3. Choose the "MATCH COOK" for second basket, and press the "START/PAUSE" to start cooking. Flip the salmon once cooked halfway through. Serve!

Nutrition: Calories: 275; Fat: 1g; Carbs: 31g; Protein: 29g

Cod Fish Nuggets

Preparation time: 10 minutes
Cooking time: 12 minutes
Servings: 4

Ingredients:
- 454g cod, cut into bite-size pieces
- 32g all-purpose flour
- 2g salt
- 2g black pepper
- 2 eggs
- 128g panko breadcrumbs
- 2g garlic powder

Directions:
1. Mix the pepper, salt, and flour in a bowl. Whisk two eggs in another bowl. Mix the garlic powder and breadcrumbs in the third bowl.
2. Coat the cod pieces in the flour mixture, and dip it in the egg. Then, coat it in the panko mixture.
3. Divide the cod mixture into two air fryer baskets. Place both baskets in your air fryer. Choose the "AIR FRY" for the first basket at 200°C and set the time to 12 minutes.
4. Choose the "MATCH COOK" for second basket, and press the "START/PAUSE" to start cooking. Serve!

Nutrition: Calories: 190; Fat: 5g; Carbs: 17g; Protein: 24g

Cajun Fried Catfish

Preparation time: 15 minutes + marinating time
Cooking time: 20 minutes
Servings: 2

Ingredients:
- 454g catfish fillets
- few dashes of hot sauce
- 64g yellow cornmeal
- 29g all-purpose flour
- 5g Cajun seasoning
- 2g lemon pepper seasoning
- salt & fresh cracked black pepper, to taste

Directions:
1. Mix the hot sauce and catfish fillets in a bowl, then let it sit for 30 minutes.
2. Meanwhile, mix the seasonings, black pepper, flour, and cornmeal on a plate.
3. Remove the catfish fillets from the hot sauce and season with salt. Dredge it in cornmeal mixture until well coated.
4. Divide the catfish mixture into two air fryer baskets. Place both baskets in your air fryer. Choose the "AIR

FRY" for the first basket at 200°C and set the time to 20 minutes.
5. Choose the "MATCH COOK" for second basket, and press the "START/PAUSE" to start cooking. Serve!

Nutrition: Calories: 208; Fat: 9g; Carbs: 8g; Protein: 17g

Coconut Shrimp

Preparation time: 10 minutes
Cooking time: 10 minutes
Servings: 4

Ingredients:
- 454g raw shrimp, peeled and deveined with tail on
- 2 eggs, beaten
- 64g all-purpose flour
- 64g unsweetened coconut, shredded
- 32g panko breadcrumbs
- 5g salt
- 1g black pepper

Directions:
1. Add the flour to one bowl. Add the egg to another bowl and beat it well. Mix the black pepper, salt, breadcrumbs, and coconut in a third bowl.
2. Coat the shrimp in flour and then dredge in the egg. Dip in the coconut mixture until covered.
3. Divide the shrimp into two air fryer baskets. Place both baskets in your air fryer. Choose the "AIR FRY" for the first basket at 198°C and set the time to 10 minutes.
4. Choose the "MATCH COOK" for second basket, and press the "START/PAUSE" to start cooking. Serve!

Nutrition: Calories: 293; Fat: 11g; Carbs: 17g; Protein: 28g

Air Fried Mussels

Preparation time: 10 minutes
Cooking time: 5 minutes
Servings: 4

Ingredients:
- 450g mussels, soak in water for 30 minutes & cleaned
- 14ml butter
- 230ml water
- 10g garlic, minced
- 5g chives, chopped
- 5g basil, chopped
- 5g parsley, chopped

Directions:
1. Mix the mussels, parsley, basil, chives, butter, garlic, and water into the bowl. Divide the mussel mixture into two air fryer baskets.
2. Place both baskets in your air fryer. Choose the "AIR FRY" for the first basket at 120°C and set the time to 5 minutes.
3. Choose the "MATCH COOK" for second basket, and press the "START/PAUSE" to start cooking. Serve!

Nutrition: Calories: 223; Fat: 3g; Carbs: 9g; Protein: 27g

Marinated Prawns

Preparation time: 10 minutes + marinating time
Cooking time: 8 minutes
Servings: 4

Ingredients:
- 400g king prawns, peeled, uncooked
- half of 1 onion, chopped
- 2 cloves of garlic, chopped
- 5g parsley, chopped
- 30ml olive oil
- half of a lemon to serve
- 1 pinch of sea salt & black pepper

Directions:
1. Mix the parsley, garlic, onions, and prawns in a large bowl. Let it marinate for 15 minutes. Divide the prawn mixture into two air fryer baskets.
2. Place both baskets in your air fryer. Choose the "AIR FRY" for the first basket at 220°C and set the time to 8 minutes.
3. Choose the "MATCH COOK" for second basket, and press the "START/PAUSE" to start cooking. When done, squeeze the lemon juice on top before serving.

Nutrition: Calories: 317; Fat: 17g; Carbs: 6g; Protein: 42g

Crab Cakes

Preparation time: 10 minutes
Cooking time: 10 minutes
Servings: 4

Ingredients:
- 227g lump crab meat
- 1 red capsicum, chopped
- 3 green onions, chopped
- 3 tbsp mayonnaise
- 3 tbsp breadcrumbs
- 2 tsp old bay seasoning
- 1 tsp lemon juice

Directions:
1. Process all the fixings in a food processor. Make the crab cakes out of this mixture. Divide the crab cakes into the two air fryer baskets.
2. Place both baskets in your air fryer. Choose the "AIR FRY" for the first basket at 177°C and set the time to 10 minutes.
3. Choose the "MATCH COOK" for second basket, and press the "START/PAUSE" to start cooking. Flip the crab cakes once cooked halfway through. Serve!

Nutrition: Calories: 163; Fat: 11g; Carbs: 8g; Protein: 7g

Sesame Jumbo Shrimp

Preparation time: 10 minutes

Cooking time: 10 minutes
Servings: 4-5

Ingredients:
- 15 jumbo shrimp, deveined, rinsed, and pat dried
- 14ml olive oil
- 22ml soy sauce
- 14g garlic, minced
- 7g sugar
- 5g Italian seasoning
- 5g ground black pepper
- 5g white sesame seeds for garnish
- 28g coriander for garnish

Directions:
1. Remove the shrimp veins and rinse under clean water. Then, pat dries it with a paper towel.
2. Add the shrimp into the bowl with black pepper, Italian seasoning, sugar, garlic, soy sauce, and olive oil. Cover, and let it rest for 20 minutes.
3. Divide the shrimp into two air fryer baskets. Choose the "AIR FRY" for the first basket at 176°C and set the time to 10 minutes.
4. Choose the "MATCH COOK" for second basket, and press the "START/PAUSE" to start cooking.
5. Transfer the shrimp onto the plate—top with sesame seeds and fresh coriander before serving.

Nutrition: Calories: 107; Fat: 5g; Carbs: 4g; Protein: 10g

Crab Stuffed Mushrooms

Preparation time: 15 minutes
Cooking time: 18 minutes
Servings: 4

Ingredients:
- 907g baby Bella mushrooms
- 227g lump crab
- 2 tsp salt
- One-fourth of 1 red onion, diced
- 2 celery ribs, diced
- 50g seasoned bread crumbs
- 1 large egg
- 60g parmesan cheese, shredded
- 1 tsp oregano
- 1 tsp hot sauce
- cooking spray

Directions:
1. Mix all the fixings except the mushrooms in a bowl. Divide it into your mushroom caps. Place the caps among the two air fryer baskets.
2. Place both baskets in your air fryer. Choose the "AIR FRY" for the first basket at 200°C and set the time to 18 minutes.
3. Choose the "MATCH COOK" for second basket, and press the "START/PAUSE" to start cooking. Serve!

Nutrition: Calories: 399; Fat: 16g; Carbs: 28g; Protein: 35g

Shrimp Skewers

Preparation time: 10 minutes
Cooking time: 10 minutes
Servings: 4

Ingredients:
- 453g shrimp
- 15ml lemon juice

- 15ml olive oil
- 1 tbsp old bay seasoning
- 1 tsp garlic, minced

Directions:
1. Toss the shrimp with old bay seasoning, garlic, lemon juice, and olive oil in your bowl. Thread the shrimp onto the soaked skewers.
2. Insert a crisper plate in the air fryer baskets. Place the shrimp skewers in both air fryer baskets. Choose the "AIR FRY" for the first basket at 198°C and set the time to 10 minutes.
3. Choose the "MATCH COOK" for second basket, and press the "START/PAUSE" to start cooking. Serve!

Nutrition: Calories: 167; Fat: 5g; Carbs: 2g; Protein: 25g

Herb Lemon Mussels

Preparation time: 10 minutes
Cooking time: 10 minutes
Servings: 6

Ingredients:
- 1 kg. mussels, steamed & half shell
- 1 tbsp thyme, chopped
- 1 tbsp parsley, chopped
- 1 tsp dried parsley
- 1 tsp garlic, minced
- 60ml olive oil
- 45ml lemon juice
- salt & pepper to taste

Directions:
1. Mix all the fixings in your bowl.
2. Insert a crisper plate in the air fryer baskets. Add the mussels to both baskets.
3. Choose the "AIR FRY" for the first basket at 182°C and set the time to 10 minutes.
4. Choose the "MATCH COOK" for second basket, and press the "START/PAUSE" to start cooking. Serve!

Nutrition: Calories: 206; Fat: 11g; Carbs: 6g; Protein: 18g

SIDES RECIPES

Acorn Squash Slices

Preparation time: 15 minutes
Cooking time: 10 minutes
Servings: 6

Ingredients:
- 2 medium acorn squashes, halved, seeded & sliced into 1.27-cm slices
- 96g packed brown sugar
- 113g butter, melted

Directions:
1. Divide the squash slices into the air fryer baskets. Drizzle brown sugar and butter over the squash slices.
2. Place both baskets in your air fryer. Choose the "AIR FRY" for the first basket at 177°C and set the time to 10 minutes.
3. Choose the "MATCH COOK" for second basket, and press the "START/PAUSE" to start cooking. Flip the squash once cooked halfway through. Serve!

Nutrition: Calories: 206; Fat: 3g; Carbs: 35g; Protein: 10g

Peppered Asparagus

Preparation time: 10 minutes
Cooking time: 16 minutes
Servings: 6

Ingredients:
- 1 bunch of asparagus, trimmed
- 15ml avocado or olive oil spray
- Himalayan salt &black pepper to taste

Directions:
1. Divide the asparagus into two air fryer baskets. Toss the asparagus with salt, black pepper, and oil.
2. Place both baskets in your air fryer. Choose the "AIR FRY" for the first basket at 200°C and set the time to 16 minutes.
3. Choose the "MATCH COOK" for second basket, and press the "START/PAUSE" to start cooking. Serve!

Nutrition: Calories: 163; Fat: 11g; Carbs: 8g; Protein: 7g

Green Tomato Stacks

Preparation time: 15 minutes
Cooking time: 12 minutes
Servings: 6
Ingredients:
- 2 medium green tomatoes, cut into 4 slices
- 2 medium tomatoes, cut into 4 slices
- 58g mayonnaise
- .25 tsp lime zest, grated
- 2 tbsp lime juice
- 1 tsp minced fresh thyme
- 31g all-purpose flour
- 2 large egg whites, beaten
- 92g cornmeal
- .50 tsp black pepper
- .25 tsp salt
- Cooking spray
- 8 slices Canadian bacon, warmed

Directions:
1. Mix the mayonnaise with .25 tsp black pepper, thyme, lime juice and zest in a bowl.
2. Spread the flour in one bowl, beat the egg whites in another, and mix cornmeal with .25 tsp black pepper and salt in a third bowl.
3. Coat each tomato with the flour, then in the egg whites. Lastly, in the cornmeal mixture.
4. Divide the tomato slices into the two air fryer baskets. Place both baskets in your air fryer. Choose the "AIR FRY" for the first basket at 199°C and set the time to 12 minutes.
5. Choose the "MATCH COOK" for second basket, and press the "START/PAUSE" to start cooking.
6. Flip the tomatoes once cooked halfway through. Place the green tomato slices on the working surface. Top them with bacon and a red tomato slice. Serve.

Nutrition: Calories: 113; Fat: 3g; Carbs: 20g; Protein: 3g

Bacon Wrapped Corn Cob

Preparation time: 15 minutes
Cooking time: 10 minutes
Servings: 4

Ingredients:
- 4 trimmed corns on the cob
- 8 bacon slices

Directions:
1. Wrap the corn cobs with two bacon slices. Divide the wrapped cobs into the two air fryer baskets.
2. Place both baskets in your air fryer. Choose the "AIR FRY" for the first basket at 180°C and set the time to 10 minutes.
3. Choose the "MATCH COOK" for second basket, and press the "START/PAUSE" to start cooking. Flip the corn cob once cooked halfway through. Serve!

Nutrition: Calories: 350; Fat: 3g; Carbs: 64g; Protein: 19g

Stuffed Tomatoes

Preparation time: 15 minutes
Cooking time: 8 minutes
Servings: 2

Ingredients:
- 400g brown rice, cooked
- 260g tofu, grilled and chopped
- 4 large red tomatoes, cored
- 4 tbsp basil, chopped
- .25 tbsp olive oil
- Salt & black pepper, to taste
- 2 tbsp lemon juice
- 1 tsp red chilli powder
- 45g Parmesan cheese

Directions:
1. Mix the rice, tofu, basil, olive oil, salt, black pepper, lemon juice, and chilli powder in a large bowl.
2. Fill each tomato with the rice mixture. Sprinkle it with cheese on top.
3. Divide the stuffed tomatoes into two air fryer baskets. Place both

baskets in your air fryer. Choose the "AIR FRY" for the first basket at 200°C and set the time to 8 minutes.
4. Choose the "MATCH COOK" for second basket, and press the "START/PAUSE" to start cooking. Serve!

Nutrition: Calories: 245; Fat: 1g; Carbs: 48g; Protein: 11g

Garlic-Rosemary Brussels Sprouts

Preparation time: 15 minutes
Cooking time: 8 minutes
Servings: 4

Ingredients:
- 3 tbsp olive oil
- 2 garlic cloves, minced
- .50 tsp salt
- .25 tsp black pepper
- 455g Brussels sprouts, halved
- 50g panko bread crumbs
- 1.50 tsp rosemary, minced

Directions:
1. Mix all the fixings in a bowl. Divide the sprouts into two air fryer baskets.
2. Place both baskets in your air fryer. Choose the "AIR FRY" for the first basket at 177°C and set the time to 8 minutes.
3. Choose the "MATCH COOK" for second basket, and press the "START/PAUSE" to start cooking. Serve!

Nutrition: Calories: 231; Fat: 9g; Carbs: 32g; Protein: 6g

Onion Rings

Preparation time: 10 minutes
Cooking time: 7 minutes
Servings: 4

Ingredients:
- 170g onion, sliced into rings
- 30g breadcrumbs
- 2 eggs, beaten
- 65g flour
- Salt & black pepper to taste

Directions:
1. Mix the flour with the black pepper plus salt in your bowl.
2. Dredge the onion rings through the flour mixture, then in the eggs and lastly, in the breadcrumbs.
3. Divide the coated onion rings into two air fryer baskets. Place both baskets in your air fryer. Choose the "AIR FRY" for the first basket at 177°C and set the time to 7 minutes.
4. Choose the "MATCH COOK" for second basket, and press the "START/PAUSE" to start cooking. Serve!

Nutrition: Calories: 185; Fat: 11g; Carbs: 21g; Protein: 4g

Balsamic Vegetables

Preparation time: 10 minutes + marinating time
Cooking time: 12 minutes
Servings: 4

Ingredients:
- 125g asparagus, cut woody ends
- 88g mushrooms, halved
- 170g grape tomatoes
- 1 courgette, sliced
- 1 yellow squash, sliced
- 1 tbsp Dijon mustard
- 3 tbsp soy sauce
- 27g brown sugar
- 57ml balsamic vinegar
- 32g olive oil
- salt & pepper to taste

Directions:
1. Mix the asparagus, tomatoes, oil, mustard, soy sauce, mushrooms, zucchini, squash, brown sugar, vinegar, pepper, and salt in a bowl. Cover and place it in the fridge for 45 minutes.
2. Insert a crisper plate in the air fryer baskets. Add the vegetable mixture to both baskets.
3. Choose the "AIR FRY" for the first basket at 199°C and set the time to 12 minutes.
4. Choose the "MATCH COOK" for second basket, and press the "START/PAUSE" to start cooking. Stir halfway through. Serve!

Nutrition: Calories: 184; Fat: 13g; Carbs: 14g; Protein: 5g

Air-Fried Asparagus

Preparation time: 5 minutes
Cooking time: 6 minutes
Servings: 4
Ingredients:
- 58g mayonnaise
- 4 tsp olive oil
- 1.50 tsp grated lemon zest
- 1 garlic clove, minced
- .50 tsp pepper
- .25 tsp seasoned salt
- 2 tbsp shredded parmesan cheese

Directions:
1. Combine the mayonnaise, olive oil, lemon zest, garlic clove, pepper, and salt in a large bowl. Add the asparagus, and toss to coat.
2. Insert a crisper plate in both air fryer baskets. Divide the asparagus into one layer in each drawer. Top with parmesan cheese.
3. Place both baskets in your air fryer. Choose the "AIR FRY" for the first basket at 191°C and set the time to 6 minutes.
4. Choose the "MATCH COOK" for second basket, and press the "START/PAUSE" to start cooking. Serve!

Nutrition: Calories: 156; Fat: 15g; Carbs: 3g; Protein: 2g

Mexican Cauliflower

Preparation time: 10 minutes
Cooking time: 12 minutes
Servings: 4

Ingredients:
- 1 medium cauliflower head, cut into florets
- .50 tsp turmeric
- 1 tsp onion powder
- 2 tsp garlic powder
- 2 tsp parsley
- 1 lime juice
- 30ml olive oil
- 1 tsp chilli powder
- 1 tsp cumin
- salt & pepper to taste

Directions:
1. Toss the cauliflower florets in a bowl with onion powder, garlic powder, parsley, oil, chilli powder, turmeric, cumin, pepper, and salt.
2. Insert a crisper plate in both air fryer baskets. Divide the cauliflower florets into both baskets. Place it in your air fryer.
3. Choose the "AIR FRY" for the first basket at 199°C and set the time to 12 minutes.
4. Choose the "MATCH COOK" for second basket, and press the "START/PAUSE" to start cooking. Stir halfway through—drizzle lime juice over cauliflower florets. Serve!

Nutrition: Calories: 108; Fat: 7g; Carbs: 10g; Protein: 3g

Air Fried Okra

Preparation time: 10 minutes
Cooking time: 13 minutes
Servings: 2

Ingredients:
- 227g okra pods, sliced
- 1 tsp olive oil
- .25 tsp salt
- black pepper to taste

Directions:
1. Toss the okra with olive oil, salt, plus black pepper in your bowl. Spread the okra in one layer into the two air fryer baskets.
2. Place both baskets in your air fryer. Choose the "AIR FRY" for the first basket at 191°C and set the time to 13 minutes.
3. Choose the "MATCH COOK" for second basket, and press the "START/PAUSE" to start cooking.
4. Toss the okra once cooked halfway through, and resume cooking. Serve!

Nutrition: Calories: 208; Fat: 5g; Carbs: 34g; Protein: 5g

Breaded Summer Squash

Preparation time: 15 minutes
Cooking time: 10 minutes
Servings: 4
Ingredients:
- 4 cups yellow summer squash, sliced
- 3 tablespoons olive oil
- .50 tsp salt
- .50 tsp pepper
- .12 tsp cayenne pepper
- 75 panko bread crumbs
- 67g grated Parmesan cheese

Directions:
1. Mix the breadcrumbs, cheese, cayenne pepper, black pepper, salt and oil in a bowl. Coat the squash slices with the breadcrumb mixture.
2. Divide these slices into the two air fryer baskets. Place both baskets in your air fryer. Choose the "AIR FRY" for the first basket at 177°C and set the time to 10 minutes.
3. Choose the "MATCH COOK" for second basket, and press the "START/PAUSE" to start cooking.
4. Flip the squash slices once cooked halfway through. Serve!

Nutrition: Calories: 193; Fat: 1g; Carbs: 38g; Protein: 6g

BBQ Sriracha Baby Corn

Preparation time: 10 minutes
Cooking time: 10 minutes
Servings: 4
Ingredients:
- 450g can baby corn, drained & rinsed
- 50g BBQ sauce
- .50 tsp Sriracha sauce

Directions:
1. Toss the baby corn with sriracha sauce and BBQ sauce in a bowl until well coated.
2. Insert a crisper plate in the air fryer baskets. Add the baby corn to both baskets.
3. Choose the "AIR FRY" for the first basket at 200°C and set the time to 10 minutes.
4. Choose the "MATCH COOK" for second basket and press the "START/PAUSE" to start cooking. Stir halfway through. Serve!

Nutrition: Calories: 46; Fat: 0g; Carbs: 10g; Protein: 0g

Rosemary Asparagus & Potatoes

Preparation time: 10 minutes
Cooking time: 30 minutes
Servings: 6
Ingredients:
- 150g asparagus, trimmed & cut into pieces
- 2 tsp garlic powder
- 2 tbsp rosemary, chopped
- 30ml olive oil
- 700g baby potatoes, quartered
- .50 tsp red pepper flakes
- salt & pepper to taste

Directions:
1. Insert a crisper plate in the air fryer baskets.
2. Toss the potatoes with 1 tbsp oil, pepper, and salt in a bowl until well coated. Add the potatoes into in zone 1 basket.

3. Toss the asparagus with the remaining oil, red pepper flakes, pepper, garlic powder, and rosemary in a bowl. Add the asparagus into the zone 2 basket.
4. Choose the "AIR FRY" for the first basket at 200°C and set the time to 20 minutes.
5. Choose the "AIR FRY" for the second basket at 200°C and set the time to 10 minutes. Press the "START/PAUSE" to start cooking. Serve!

Nutrition: Calories: 121; Fat: 5g; Carbs: 17g; Protein: 4g

Courgette With Broccoli

Preparation time: 15 minutes
Cooking time: 15 minutes
Servings: 2
Ingredients:
- 1 courgette, diced
- 2 capsicums, diced
- 1 head of broccoli, diced
- 1 red onion, diced
- 1 tsp each of smoked paprika, garlic granules, & Herb de Provence
- Salt & black pepper, to taste
- 1.50 tbsp olive oil
- 2 tbsp lemon juice

Directions:
1. Toss all the fixings in a bowl. Divide the vegetables into the two air fryer baskets.
2. Place both baskets in your air fryer. Choose the "AIR FRY" for the first basket at 200°C and set the time to 15 minutes.
3. Choose the "MATCH COOK" for second basket and press the "START/PAUSE" to start cooking. Serve!

Nutrition: Calories: 166; Fat: 3g; Carbs: 28g; Protein: 5g

VEGAN RECIPES

Carrot Fries

Preparation time: 5 minutes
Cooking time: 10 minutes
Servings: 4

Ingredients:
- 454g carrots, peeled & cut into fries
- 10ml olive oil
- 2g garlic salt

Directions:
1. Toss the carrots with the garlic salt and oil into a bowl. Divide the fries into two air fryer baskets.
2. Place both baskets in your air fryer. Choose the "BAKE" for the first basket at 200°C and set the time to 10 minutes.
3. Choose the "MATCH COOK" for second basket, and press the "START/PAUSE" to start cooking. Serve!

Nutrition: Calories: 60; Fat: 2g; Carbs: 9g; Protein: 1g

Air Fried Mixed Vegetables

Preparation time: 10 minutes
Cooking time: 15 minutes
Servings: 4

Ingredients:
- 52g onion, sliced
- 71g broccoli florets
- 116g radishes, sliced
- 15ml olive oil
- 100g Brussels sprouts, cut in half
- 325g cauliflower florets
- 1 tsp balsamic vinegar
- .50 tsp garlic powder
- salt & pepper to taste

Directions:
1. Toss the vegetables with oil, vinegar, garlic powder, pepper, and salt in a bowl.
2. Insert a crisper plate in the air fryer baskets, and add the vegetables to both baskets.
3. Place both baskets in your air fryer. Choose the "AIR FRY" for the first basket at 193°C and set the time to 15 minutes.
4. Choose the "MATCH COOK" for second basket, and press the "START/PAUSE" to start cooking. Serve!

Nutrition: Calories: 71; Fat: 3g; Carbs: 8g; Protein: 3g

Beet Chips

Preparation time: 15 minutes
Cooking time: 25 minutes
Servings: 4

Ingredients:
- 680g beet, cut into thick slices
- 10ml rapeseed oil
- 1g salt
- 1g black pepper

Directions:
1. Combine the pepper, salt, oil, and sliced beets in a large bowl. Divide it into two air fryer baskets.
2. Place both baskets in your air fryer. Choose the "AIR FRY" for the first

basket at 160°C and set the time to 25 minutes.
3. Choose the "MATCH COOK" for second basket, and press the "START/PAUSE" to start cooking. Serve!

Nutrition: Calories: 47; Fat: 2g; Carbs: 6g; Protein: 1g

Sweet Potatoes with Carrots

Preparation time: 10 minutes
Cooking time: 25 minutes
Servings: 8

Ingredients:
- 453g carrots, sliced
- 2 tsp smoked paprika
- 21g sugar
- 30ml olive oil
- 453g potatoes, diced
- .25 tsp thyme
- .50 tsp dried oregano
- 1 tsp garlic powder
- salt & pepper to taste

Directions:
1. Toss the carrots and potatoes with 1 tablespoon of oil in a bowl.
2. Insert a crisper plate in the air fryer baskets. Divide the carrots and potatoes into both baskets.
3. Place both baskets in your air fryer. Choose the "AIR FRY" for the first basket at 199°C and set the time to 15 minutes.
4. Choose the "MATCH COOK" for second basket, and press the "START/PAUSE" to start cooking.
5. In a mixing bowl, add the cooked potatoes, carrots, smoked paprika, sugar, oil, thyme, oregano, garlic powder, pepper, and salt and toss well.
6. Return the carrot and potato mixture to two air fryer baskets and cook for 10 minutes more.

Nutrition: Calories: 101; Fat: 4g; Carbs: 16g; Protein: 2g

Fried Mushrooms

Preparation time: 10 minutes + chilling time
Cooking time: 10-12 minutes
Serving: 4

Ingredients:
- 170g oyster mushrooms, rinsed and dried, broken into large pieces
- 59ml almond milk
- 14g yellow mustard
- 5ml hot sauce
- 64g all-purpose flour
- 5g seasoned salt
- 5g garlic powder
- 5g onion powder
- 5g Italian seasoning
- 2g cayenne pepper

Directions:
1. Whisk the hot sauce, mustard, and almond milk into a shallow bowl. Keep it aside.
2. Whisk the cayenne pepper, Italian seasoning, onion powder, garlic powder, seasoned flour, and all-purpose flour into the bowl.
3. Coat each mushroom piece in the milk mixture and then coat in the flour mixture. Place the coated

pieces onto the plate. Put it into the refrigerator for 20 minutes.
4. Divide the mushroom into two air fryer baskets. Place both baskets in your air fryer. Choose the "AIR FRY" for the first basket at 200°C and set the time to 10 to 12 minutes.
5. Choose the "MATCH COOK" for second basket, and press the "START/PAUSE" to start cooking. Serve!

Nutrition: Calories: 91; Fat: 2g; Carbs: 16g; Protein: 4g

Broccoli & Squash with Peppers

Preparation time: 10 minutes
Cooking time: 12 minutes
Servings: 4

Ingredients:
- 175g broccoli florets
- 1 red bell pepper, diced
- 1 tbsp olive oil
- .50 tsp garlic powder
- one-fourth of 1 onion, sliced
- 1 zucchini, sliced
- 2 yellow squashes, sliced
- salt & pepper to taste

Directions:
1. Toss the vegetable with oil, pepper, garlic powder, and salt in your bowl.
2. Insert a crisper plate in the air fryer baskets. Add the vegetable mixture to both baskets.
3. Place both baskets in your air fryer. Choose the "AIR FRY" for the first basket at 199°C and set the time to 12 minutes.
4. Choose the "MATCH COOK" for second basket, and press the "START/PAUSE" to start cooking. Serve!

Nutrition: Calories: 75; Fat: 4g; Carbs: 10g; Protein: 3g

Sesame Kale Chips

Preparation time: 10 minutes
Cooking time: 28 minutes
Serving: 2

Ingredients:
- 768g kale leaves, stems & ribs removed
- 14ml olive oil
- 5ml low-sodium tamari
- 5g white or black sesame seeds
- 2.5g garlic, minced
- 1g poppy seeds

Instructions:
1. Rinse and dry kale leaves and then tear them into pieces. Add the tamari, olive oil, and kale into the bowl and toss to combine.
2. Divide the kale into two air fryer baskets. Place both baskets in your air fryer. Choose the "AIR FRY" for the first basket at 190°C and set the time to 28 minutes.
3. Choose the "MATCH COOK" for second basket, and press the "START/PAUSE" to start cooking.
4. Open the lid, sprinkle with poppy seeds, garlic, and sesame seeds and close the lid. Serve!

Nutrition: Calories: 159; Fat: 8g; Carbs: 20g; Protein: 7g

Potatoes with Green Beans

Preparation time: 10 minutes
Cooking time: 25 minutes
Servings: 4

Ingredients:
- 453g potatoes, cut into pieces
- 15ml olive oil
- 1 tsp garlic powder
- 160g green beans, trimmed
- salt & pepper to taste

Directions:
1. Toss all the fixings in your bowl.
2. Insert a crisper plate in the air fryer baskets. Divide the green beans and potato mixture into both baskets.
3. Place both baskets in your air fryer. Choose the "AIR FRY" for the first basket at 193°C and set the time to 25 minutes.
4. Choose the "MATCH COOK" for second basket, and press the "START/PAUSE" to start cooking. halfway through. Serve!

Nutrition: Calories: 128; Fat: 4g; Carbs: 22g; Protein: 3g

Fried Patty Pan Squash

Preparation time: 10 minutes
Cooking time: 15 minutes
Servings: 6
Ingredients:
- 565g small pattypan squash, halved
- 1 tbsp olive oil
- 2 garlic cloves, minced
- .50 tsp salt
- .25 tsp dried oregano
- .25 tsp dried thyme
- .25 tsp pepper
- 1 tbsp minced parsley

Directions:
1. Rub the squash with oil, garlic and the remaining ingredients. Spread the squash into the two air fryer baskets.
2. Place both baskets in your air fryer. Choose the "AIR FRY" for the first basket at 191°C and set the time to 15 minutes.
3. Choose the "MATCH COOK" for second basket, and press the "START/PAUSE" to start cooking.
4. Flip the squash once cooked halfway through. Garnish with parsley. Serve!

Nutrition: Calories: 208; Fat: 5g; Carbs: 34g; Protein: 5g

Potato Chips

Preparation time: 10 minutes + soaking time
Cooking time: 16 minutes
Servings: 4

Ingredients:
- 2 large potatoes, peeled and sliced
- 1.50 tsp salt
- 1.50 tsp black pepper
- Oil for misting

Directions:
1. Soak the potatoes in cold water for 30 minutes, then drain. Pat dry the potato slices and toss them with cracked pepper, salt and oil mist.
2. Divide the potatoes into the two air fryer baskets. Place both baskets in your air fryer. Choose the "AIR FRY" for the first basket at 150°C and set the time to 16 minutes.
3. Choose the "MATCH COOK" for second basket, and press the "START/PAUSE" to start cooking. Serve!

Nutrition: Calories: 122; Fat: 2g; Carbs: 17g; Protein: 14g

Cinnamon Sugar Chickpeas

Preparation time: 10 minutes
Cooking time: 15 minutes
Servings: 4
Ingredients:
- 340g chickpeas, drained
- 1 tbsp olive oil
- 1 tbsp coconut sugar
- .50 tsp cinnamon

Directions:
1. Toss the chickpeas with coconut sugar, cinnamon and oil in a bowl. Divide the chickpeas into two air fryer baskets.
2. Place both baskets in your air fryer. Choose the "AIR FRY" for the first basket at 193°C and set the time to 15 minutes.
3. Choose the "MATCH COOK" for second basket, and press the "START/PAUSE" to start cooking.
4. Toss the chickpeas once cooked halfway through. Serve!

Nutrition: Calories: 103; Fat: 7g; Carbs: 4g; Protein: 5g

Vegetable Chips

Preparation time: 10 minutes
Cooking time: 10 minutes
Servings: 2
Ingredients:
- half of 1 courgette, sliced into rounds
- half of 1 sweet potato, sliced into rounds
- 1 beet, sliced into rounds
- 5ml extra-virgin olive oil
- 1g salt
- ground black pepper, to taste

Directions:
1. Mix all the fixings in your bowl.
2. Divide the vegetable slices into two air fryer baskets. Place both baskets in your air fryer. Choose the "AIR FRY" for the first basket at 182°C and set the time to 15 minutes.
3. Choose the "MATCH COOK" for second basket, and press the "START/PAUSE" to start cooking. Serve!

Nutrition: Calories: 79; Fat: 0g; Carbs: 16g; Protein: 3g

Oregano Radishes

Preparation time: 10 minutes
Cooking time: 15 minutes
Servings: 6
Ingredients:
- 1kg radishes, quartered
- 3 tbsp olive oil
- 1 tbsp fresh oregano, minced
- .25 tsp salt
- black pepper to taste

Directions:
1. Toss the radishes with oil, black pepper, salt and oregano in a bowl. Divide the radishes into the two air fryer baskets.
2. Place both baskets in your air fryer. Choose the "AIR FRY" for the first basket at 191°C and set the time to 15 minutes.
3. Choose the "MATCH COOK" for second basket and press the "START/PAUSE" to start cooking. Toss the radishes once cooked halfway through. Serve!

Nutrition: Calories: 270; Fat: 14g; Carbs: 3g; Protein: 6g

Herb and Lemon Cauliflower

Preparation time: 10 minutes
Cooking time: 10 minutes
Servings: 4

Ingredients:
- half of cauliflower head, sliced into florets
- 7g fresh parsley
- 2 tbsp olive oil
- 1 tbsp lemon juice
- .50 tbsp each of fresh rosemary & thyme
- .50 tsp grated lemon zest
- .25 tsp salt
- crushed red pepper flakes to taste

Directions:
1. Toss the cauliflower with oil, herbs and remaining ingredients in a bowl. Divide the seasoned cauliflower into the two air fryer baskets.
2. Place both baskets in your air fryer. Choose "AIR FRY" for the first basket at 180°C and set the time to 10 minutes.
3. Choose the "MATCH COOK" for second basket and press the "START/PAUSE" to start cooking. Serve!

Nutrition: Calories: 212; Fat: 11g; Carbs: 24g; Protein: 7g

Sweet Potatoes with Brussels Sprouts

Preparation time: 10 minutes
Cooking time: 35 minutes
Servings: 8

Ingredients:
- 340g sweet potatoes, cubed
- 30ml olive oil
- 150g onion, cut into pieces
- 352g Brussels sprouts, halved
- salt & pepper to taste

Directions:
1. Toss the Brussels sprouts, oil, onion, sweet potatoes, pepper, and salt in a bowl.
2. Insert a crisper plate in the air fryer baskets. Divide the Brussels sprouts

and sweet potato mixture into both baskets.
3. Place both baskets in your air fryer. Choose "AIR FRY" for the first basket at 199°C and set the time to 25 minutes.
4. Choose the "MATCH COOK" for second basket and press the "START/PAUSE" to start cooking. Stir halfway through. Serve!

Nutrition: Calories: 142; Fat: 4g; Carbs: 25g; Protein: 3g

SNACKS AND APPETIZERS RECIPES

Parmesan Dill Chips

Preparation time: 10 minutes
Cooking time: 10 minutes
Servings: 4

Ingredients:
- 907g dill pickles, cut into thick slices
- 2 eggs
- 85g panko breadcrumbs
- 43g parmesan cheese, grated
- 1g dried dill weed

Directions:
1. Place the pickles between layers of paper towel and pat dry them. Beat the eggs into your bowl.
2. Mix the dill weed, cheese, plus breadcrumbs into your Ziplock bag.
3. Dip each pickle slice into the egg mixture and then toss the breadcrumbs mixture. Divide the coated pickle chips into two baskets.
4. Place both baskets in your air fryer. Choose "BAKE" for the first basket at 175°C and set the time to 10 minutes.
5. Choose the "MATCH COOK" for second basket and press the "START/PAUSE" to start cooking. Serve!

Nutrition: Calories: 143; Fat: 6g; Carbs: 15g; Protein: 8g

Mushroom Roll-Ups

Preparation time: 15 minutes
Cooking time: 11 minutes
Servings: 10 roll-ups

Ingredients:
- 227g portobello mushrooms, chopped
- 2 tbsp olive oil
- 1 tsp dried oregano
- 1 tsp dried thyme
- .50 tsp crushed red pepper flakes
- .25 tsp salt
- 1 (227g) package of cream cheese, softened
- 113g whole-milk ricotta cheese
- 10 (20 cm) flour tortillas
- Cooking spray

Directions:
1. Sauté the mushrooms with oil, thyme, salt, pepper flakes, and oregano in a skillet for 4 minutes.
2. Mix all the cheeses, add the sauteed mushrooms the mix well. Divide the mushroom mixture over the tortillas.
3. Roll the tortillas and secure them with a toothpick. Divide the rolls into two air fryer baskets. Place both baskets in your air fryer. Choose "AIR FRY" for the first basket at 200°C and set the time to 11 minutes.
4. Choose the "MATCH COOK" for second basket and press the "START/PAUSE" to start cooking. Serve!

Nutrition: Calories: 288; Fat: 7g; Carbs: 46g; Protein: 10g

Fried Ravioli

Preparation time: 15 minutes
Cooking time: 7 minutes
Servings: 6
Ingredients:
- 12 frozen raviolis
- 118ml buttermilk
- 50g panko breadcrumbs

Directions:
1. Dip the ravioli in the buttermilk, then coat it with the breadcrumbs. Divide the ravioli into two air fryer baskets.
2. Place both baskets in your air fryer. Choose "AIR FRY" for the first basket at 200°C and set the time to 7 minutes.
3. Choose the "MATCH COOK" for second basket and press the "START/PAUSE" to start cooking. Flip the ravioli once cooked halfway through. Serve!

Nutrition: Calories: 134; Fat: 6g; Carbs: 10g; Protein: 10g

Courgette Fritters

Preparation time: 10 minutes
Cooking time: 12 minutes
Servings: 4

Ingredients:
- 2 courgettes, grated
- 14g salt
- 1 egg
- 42g flour
- 5g garlic powder
- 1g onion powder
- 1g paprika
- 1g black pepper

Directions:
1. Sprinkle 1 tbsp salt over the grated courgettes. Let it rest for 10 minutes. Squeeze the excess water from courgettes with a paper towel and pat it dry. Transfer it to a bowl.
2. Add the black pepper, paprika, onion powder, garlic powder, egg, and all-purpose flour to the zucchini and stir well.
3. Divide the zucchini mixture into the two air fryer baskets. Place both baskets in your air fryer. Choose "AIR FRY" for the first basket at 180°C and set the time to 12 minutes.
4. Choose the "MATCH COOK" for second basket and press the "START/PAUSE" to start cooking. Serve!

Nutrition: Calories: 57; Fat: 1g; Carbs: 8g; Protein: 3g

Cheesy Cauliflower Tots

Preparation time: 10 minutes

Cooking time: 12 minutes
Servings: 6

Ingredients:
- 512g cauliflower florets, steamed, drained & process into cauliflower rice
- 1 egg, beaten
- 128g cheddar cheese, shredded
- 128g parmesan cheese, grated
- 85g panko breadcrumbs
- 28g fresh chives or parsley
- salt & pepper, to taste

Directions:
1. Squeeze out excess water from the cauliflower with a paper towel.
2. Mix the ingredients into the bowl and season with pepper and salt, then form it into tater tots.
3. Divide it into two air fryer baskets. Place both baskets in your air fryer. Choose "AIR FRY" for the first basket at 200°C and set the time to 12 minutes.
4. Choose the "MATCH COOK" for second basket, and press the "START/PAUSE" to start cooking. Serve!

Nutrition: Calories: 295; Fat: 2g; Carbs: 16g; Protein: 20g

Sweet Potato Wedges

Preparation time: 10 minutes
Cooking time: 20 minutes
Servings: 4
Ingredients:
- 2 sweet potatoes, peel & cut into wedges
- 1 tbsp BBQ spice rub
- .50 tsp sweet paprika
- 1 tbsp olive oil
- salt & pepper to taste

Directions:
1. Toss the sweet potato wedges with sweet paprika, oil, BBQ spice rub, pepper, and salt in a bowl.
2. Insert a crisper plate in the air fryer baskets. Divide the sweet potato wedges into both baskets.
3. Place both baskets in your air fryer. Choose "AIR FRY" for the first basket at 199°C and set the time to 20 minutes.
4. Choose the "MATCH COOK" for second basket, and press the "START/PAUSE" to start cooking. Turn it halfway through. Serve!

Nutrition: Calories: 87; Fat: 4g; Carbs: 13g; Protein: 1g

Veggie Quesadillas

Preparation time: 10 minutes
Cooking time: 20 minutes
Servings: 4

Ingredients:
- 4 whole-grain flour tortillas
- 64g low-fat cheese, shredded
- 128g red bell pepper, sliced
- 128g zucchini, sliced
- 128g black beans, drained and rinsed
- 28g fresh coriander, chopped

Directions:
1. Place the tortillas onto the clean work surface. Top it with 2 tbsp shredded cheese over half of each tortilla.

2. Top it with black beans, zucchini slices, red pepper slices, and 64g of cheese. Fold over half-moon-shaped quesadillas, and coat with cooking spray.
3. Divide the quesadillas into two air fryer baskets. Place both baskets in your air fryer. Choose "AIR FRY" for the first basket at 200°C and set the time to 10 minutes.
4. Choose the "MATCH COOK" for second basket, and press the "START/PAUSE" to start cooking. Cut quesadilla into wedges and garnish with coriander. Serve!

Nutrition: Calories: 291; Fat: 8g; Carbs: 36g; Protein: 17g

Kale Potato Nuggets

Preparation time: 10 minutes
Cooking time: 15 minutes
Servings: 4

Ingredients:
- 279g potatoes, chopped, boiled & mashed
- 268g kale, chopped
- 1 garlic clove, minced
- 30ml milk
- salt & pepper to taste

Directions:
1. Mix the potatoes, kale, milk, garlic, pepper, and salt in a bowl until well combined.
2. Insert a crisper plate in the air fryer baskets. Make the nuggets from this mixture, and divide it into your two air fryer baskets.
3. Place both baskets in your air fryer. Choose "AIR FRY" for the first basket at 199°C and set the time to 15 minutes.
4. Choose the "MATCH COOK" for second basket, and press the "START/PAUSE" to start cooking. Turn halfway through. Serve!

Nutrition: Calories: 90; Fat: 0g; Carbs: 19g; Protein: 4g

Cheese Stuffed Mushrooms

Preparation time: 10 minutes
Cooking time: 8 minutes
Servings: 4

Ingredients:
- 176g button mushrooms, clean & cut stems
- 46g sour cream
- 17g cream cheese, softened
- 50 tsp garlic powder
- 58g cheddar cheese, shredded
- salt & pepper to taste

Directions:
1. Mix all the fixings except the mushroom in your small bowl.
2. Stuff the cream cheese mixture into each mushroom and top each with cheddar cheese.
3. Insert a crisper plate in the air fryer baskets. Place the stuffed mushrooms in both baskets.
4. Place both baskets in your air fryer. Choose "AIR FRY" for the first basket at 188°C and set the time to 8 minutes.
5. Choose the "MATCH COOK" for second basket, and press the

"START/PAUSE" to start cooking. Serve!

Nutrition: Calories: 222; Fat: 19g; Carbs: 5g; Protein: 8g

Sriracha Avocado Fries

Preparation time: 5 minutes
Cooking time: 8 minutes
Servings: 4

Ingredients:
- 2 avocados, cut into 8 wedges
- 64g all-purpose flour
- 64g panko breadcrumbs
- 2 eggs
- 14ml water
- 59ml no-salt-added ketchup
- 29ml mayonnaise
- 14ml apple cider vinegar
- 14ml sriracha chili sauce
- 7g black pepper
- 1g salt

Directions:
1. Add the pepper and flour into the shallow bowl and stir well. Add water and eggs to another bowl and beat it. Add breadcrumbs to a third bowl.
2. Coat the avocado wedges in the flour, dip them in egg mixture, and coat them with breadcrumbs. Coat the avocado wedges with cooking spray.
3. Divide the avocado wedges into two air fryer baskets. Place both baskets in your air fryer.
4. Choose "AIR FRY" for the first basket at 200°C and set the time to 8 minutes.
5. Choose the "MATCH COOK" for second basket, and press the "START/PAUSE" to start cooking. Serve!
6. When done, remove the fries from the air fryer. Season it with salt.
7. Whisk the Sriracha, vinegar, mayonnaise, and ketchup into the bowl. Place the fried avocado onto the plate and top with sauce.

Nutrition: Calories: 262; Fat: 18g; Carbs: 23g; Protein: 5g

Spinach Balls

Preparation time: 10 minutes
Cooking time: 10 minutes
Servings: 4

Ingredients:
- 1 egg
- 29g breadcrumbs
- Half of 1 medium onion, chopped
- 225g spinach, blanched & chopped
- 1 carrot, peeled & grated
- 1 tbsp cornflour
- 1 tbsp nutritional yeast
- 1 tsp garlic, minced
- .50 tsp garlic powder
- salt & pepper to taste

Directions:
1. Combine the spinach and remaining ingredients in a bowl.
2. Insert a crisper plate in the air fryer baskets. Make small balls from the spinach mixture and place them in both baskets.
3. Place both baskets in your air fryer. Choose "AIR FRY" for the first basket at 199°C and set the time to 10 minutes.

4. Choose the "MATCH COOK" for second basket, and press the "START/PAUSE" to start cooking. Serve!

Nutrition: Calories: 74; Fat: 2g; Carbs: 11g; Protein: 4g

Tofu Veggie Meatballs

Preparation time: 10 minutes
Cooking time: 10 minutes
Servings: 4

Ingredients:
- 122g firm tofu, drained
- 50g breadcrumbs
- 37g bamboo shoots, thinly sliced
- 22g carrots, shredded & steamed
- 1 tsp garlic powder
- 1.50 tbsp soy sauce
- 2 tbsp cornflour
- 3 dried shitake mushrooms, soaked & chopped
- salt & pepper to taste

Directions:
1. Add all the fixings to your food processor and process until well combined.
2. Insert a crisper plate in the air fryer baskets. Make small balls from the tofu mixture and place them in both baskets.
3. Place both baskets in your air fryer. Choose "AIR FRY" for the first basket at 193°C and set the time to 10 minutes.
4. Choose the "MATCH COOK" for second basket, and press the "START/PAUSE" to start cooking. Turn halfway through. Serve!

Nutrition: Calories: 125; Fat: 2g; Carbs: 23g; Protein: 5g

Bacon Wrapped Tater Tots

Preparation time: 10 minutes
Cooking time: 14 minutes
Servings: 8

Ingredients:
- 8 bacon slices, cut each in half
- 3 tbsp honey
- .50 tbsp chipotle chilli powder
- 16 frozen tater tots

Directions:
1. Wrap each tater tot with a bacon slice. Brush the bacon with honey and drizzle chipotle chilli powder over them.
2. Insert a toothpick to seal the bacon, and divide the wrapped tots into the two air fryer baskets.
3. Place both baskets in your air fryer. Choose "AIR FRY" for the first basket at 177°C and set the time to 14 minutes.
4. Choose the "MATCH COOK" for second basket, and press the "START/PAUSE" to start cooking. Serve!

Nutrition: Calories: 100; Fat: 2g; Carbs: 4g; Protein: 18g

Cheese Corn Fritters

Preparation time: 10 minutes
Cooking time: 12 minutes
Servings: 6
Ingredients:
- 1 egg
- 164g corn
- 2 green onions, diced
- 45g flour
- 29g breadcrumbs
- 117g cheddar cheese, shredded
- .50 tsp onion powder
- .50 tsp garlic powder
- 15g sour cream
- salt & pepper to taste

Directions:
1. Mix all the fixings in a large bowl.
2. Insert a crisper plate in the air fryer baskets. Make the patties from the mixture and place them in both baskets.
3. Place both baskets in your air fryer. Choose "AIR FRY" for the first basket at 188°C and set the time to 12 minutes.
4. Choose the "MATCH COOK" for second basket, and press the "START/PAUSE" to start cooking. Turn halfway through. Serve!

Nutrition: Calories: 100; Fat: 4g; Carbs: 10g; Protein: 5g

Jalapeno Poppers

Preparation time: 15 minutes
Cooking time: 5 minutes
Servings: 5
Ingredients:
- 5 jalapenos, halves & seeded
- .25 tsp red pepper flakes, crushed
- 1 tsp each of onion powder & garlic powder
- 32g salsa
- 113g goat cheese
- salt & pepper to taste

Directions:
1. Mix the goat cheese, salsa, red pepper flakes, onion & garlic powder, pepper, plus salt in your bowl. Stuff each jalapeno half with a goat cheese mixture.
2. Insert a crisper plate in the air fryer baskets. Place the stuffed peppers in both baskets.
3. Place both baskets in your air fryer. Choose "AIR FRY" for the first basket at 182°C and set the time to 8 minutes.
4. Choose the "MATCH COOK" for second basket, and press the "START/PAUSE" to start cooking. Serve!

Nutrition: Calories: 112; Fat: 8g; Carbs: 3g; Protein: 7g

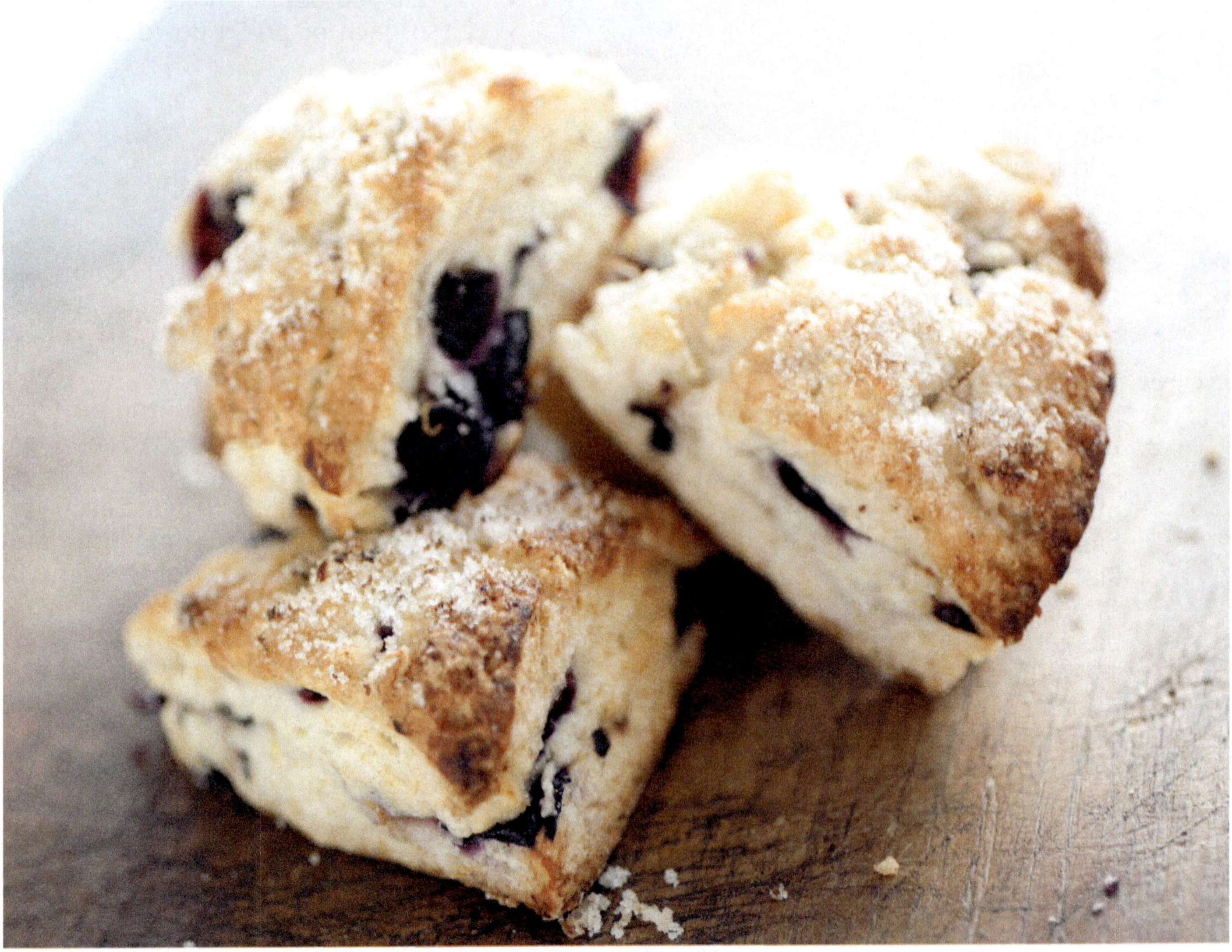

DESSERTS RECIPES

Blueberry Pie Egg Rolls

Preparation time: 10 minutes
Cooking time: 10 minutes
Servings: 12 rolls

Ingredients:
- 12 egg roll wrappers
- 190g blueberries
- 1 tbsp cornflour
- 175g agave nectar
- 1 tsp lemon zest
- 2 tbsp water
- 1 tbsp lemon juice
- Olive oil cooking spray
- Powdered sugar for dusting

Directions:
1. Mix the blueberries with cornflour, lemon zest, agave and water in a saucepan. Simmer this mixture for 5 minutes. Let it cool.
2. Spread the roll wrappers and divide the filling at the centre of the wrappers. Fold the two edges and roll each wrapper.
3. Wet and seal the wrappers, then place them in the air fryer Zone 1 basket. Spray these rolls with cooking spray.
4. Place the basket in your air fryer. Choose "AIR FRY" for the first basket at 177°C and set the time to 5 minutes.
5. Initiate cooking by pressing the "START/PAUSE" button. Dust the rolls with powdered sugar. Serve!

Nutrition: Calories: 258; Fat: 12g; Carbs: 34g; Protein: 3g

Chocolate Chip Cookies

Preparation time: 15 minutes
Cooking time: 10 minutes
Servings: 10 cookies

Ingredients:
- 76g unsalted butter, softened
- 50g granulated sugar
- 43g packed brown sugar
- .50 tsp vanilla extract
- 1 egg
- .50 tsp salt
- .50 tsp baking soda
- 96g all-purpose flour
- 109g chocolate chips
- Cooking oil in a spray

Directions:
1. Mix the butter plus sugar in your bowl until frothy. Add the vanilla extract, egg, salt, baking soda, flour, and chocolate chips. Combine to form a cookie dough.
2. Arrange a parchment paper in your air fryer baskets and scoop the cookie dough into each basket.
3. Place both baskets in your air fryer. Choose "BAKE" for the first basket at 176°C and set the time to 10 minutes.
4. Choose the "MATCH COOK" for second basket, and press the "START/PAUSE" to start cooking. Press PAUSE at the 5-minute mark to flatten and provide shape to the

cookies. Make sure they're not touching.
5. Press the START/PAUSE to resume cooking. Let it cool, and serve.

Nutrition: Calories: 140; Fat: 12g; Carbs: 4g; Protein: 2g

Roasted Oranges

Preparation time: 15 minutes
Cooking time: 6 minutes
Servings: 4

Ingredients:
- 2 oranges, halved
- 2 tsp honey
- 1 tsp cinnamon

Directions:
1. Place the oranges in each air fryer basket. Drizzle it with honey and cinnamon on top.
2. Place both baskets in your air fryer. Choose "AIR FRY" for the first basket at 200°C and set the time to 6 minutes.
3. Choose the "MATCH COOK" for second basket, and press the "START/PAUSE" to start cooking. Serve!

Nutrition: Calories: 183; Fat: 15g; Carbs: 3g; Protein: 10g

Semolina Pudding

Preparation time: 10 minutes
Cooking time: 20 minutes
Servings: 4
Ingredients:
- 45g semolina
- 1 tsp vanilla
- 500ml milk
- 115g caster sugar

Directions:
1. Mix the semolina and 250ml milk in a bowl. Slowly add the remaining milk, sugar, and vanilla, then mix well. Pour the mixture into four greased ramekins.
2. Insert a crisper plate in the air fryer baskets. Place the ramekins in both baskets.
3. Place both baskets in your air fryer. Choose "AIR FRY" for the first basket at 150°C and set the time to 20 minutes.
4. Choose the "MATCH COOK" for second basket and press the "START/PAUSE" to start cooking. Serve!

Nutrition: Calories: 209; Fat: 3g; Carbs: 41g; Protein: 6g

Apple Fritters

Preparation time: 10 minutes
Cooking time: 8 minutes
Servings: 10 fritters
Ingredients:
- 236g Bisquick baking mix
- 2 apples, peeled & diced
- 158ml milk
- 30ml butter, melted
- 1 tsp cinnamon
- 24g sugar

Directions:
1. Combine the baking mix, cinnamon, and sugar in a bowl. Pour the milk and combine you have a dough. Add the apple and stir well.
2. Insert a crisper plate in air fryer baskets. Make fritters from the mixture and place them in both baskets. Brush the fritters with melted butter.
3. Place both baskets in your air fryer. Choose "AIR FRY" for the first basket at 182°C and set the time to 10 minutes.
4. Choose the "MATCH COOK" for second basket, and press the "START/PAUSE" to start cooking. Serve!

Nutrition: Calories: 171; Fat: 7g; Carbs: 25g; Protein: 3g

Blueberry Muffins

Preparation time: 15 minutes
Cooking time: 15 minutes
Servings: 3
Ingredients:
- 1 egg
- 65g sugar
- 80ml oil
- 30ml water
- 1ml vanilla extract
- 5ml lemon zest
- 80g all-purpose flour
- 2.50g baking powder
- 75g blueberries

Directions:
1. Combine the wet ingredients in a bowl and keep it aside.
2. Whisk the dry ingredients in a small bowl. Combine both of the prepared mixture and pour it into the muffin tins.
3. Divide the muffin tins into two air fryer baskets.
4. Place the air fryer basket into the air fryer. Place both baskets in your air fryer. Choose "AIR FRY" for the first basket at 175°C and set the time to 15 minutes.
5. Choose the "MATCH COOK" for second basket, and press the "START/PAUSE" to start cooking. Serve!

Nutrition: Calories: 39; Fat: 3g; Carbs: 1g; Protein: 2g

Grilled Peaches

Preparation time: 10 minutes
Cooking time: 5 minutes
Servings: 2
Ingredients:
- 2 yellow peaches, peeled and cut into wedges
- 21g graham cracker crumbs
- 50g brown sugar
- 57g butter diced into tiny cubes

Directions:
1. Toss the peaches with crumbs, brown sugar, and butter in a bowl. Spread the peaches in Zone 1 air fryer basket.
2. Place the basket in your air fryer. Select the "AIR FRY" mode for Zone 1 with 177°C and 5 minutes of cooking time.
3. Initiate cooking by pressing the "START/PAUSE" button. Serve.

Nutrition: Calories: 327; Fat: 14g; Carbs: 47g; Protein: 4g

Pecan Pie

Preparation time: 10 minutes
Cooking time: 35 minutes
Servings: 8

Ingredients:
- 236ml light corn syrup
- 128g brown sugar
- 78ml butter, melted
- 10ml vanilla
- 2g salt
- 3 eggs
- 192g pecans, chopped
- 2 pie crusts, baked

Directions:
1. Mix the salt, vanilla, butter, sugar, plus corn syrup in your bowl. Whisk the eggs into the bowl. Add the pecans and add to the egg mixture.
2. When combined, divide the mixture into two pie crusts. Place it into the air fryer baskets.
3. Place both baskets in your air fryer. Choose "AIR FRY" for the first basket at 176°C and set the time to 35 minutes.
4. Choose the "MATCH COOK" for second basket, and press the "START/PAUSE" to start cooking. Serve!

Nutrition: Calories: 499; Fat: 22g; Carbs: 64g; Protein: 6g

Chocolate Pudding

Preparation time: 10 minutes
Cooking time: 12 minutes
Servings: 2

Ingredients:
- 1 egg
- 32g all-purpose flour
- 35g cocoa powder
- 50g sugar
- 57g butter, melted
- .50 tsp baking powder

Directions:
1. Mix all the dry fixings in your bowl. Add the egg and butter and stir until well combined. Pour the batter into the two greased ramekins.
2. Insert a crisper plate in air fryer baskets. Place the ramekins in both baskets.
3. Place both baskets in your air fryer. Choose "BAKE" for the first basket at 191°C and set the time to 12 minutes.
4. Choose the "MATCH COOK" for second basket, and press the "START/PAUSE" to start cooking. Serve!

Nutrition: Calories: 512; Fat: 27g; Carbs: 70g; Protein: 7g

Red Velvet Cookies

Preparation time: 10 minutes
Cooking time: 5 minutes
Servings: 12 cookies

Ingredients:
- 1 packet red velvet cake mix
- 2 eggs
- 118ml vegetable oil
- 96g white chocolate chips

Directions:
1. Place parchment paper into your air fryer baskets, and poke holes in the paper.
2. Combine the eggs, oil, and cake mix in a bowl until a thick dough forms.

Add the white chocolate chips and combine them with the cookie dough.
3. Divide the dough into two baskets. Place both baskets in your air fryer. Choose "AIR FRY" for the first basket at 187°C and set the time to 5 minutes.
4. Choose the "MATCH COOK" for second basket, and press the "START/PAUSE" to start cooking. Serve!

Nutrition: Calories: 305; Fat: 2g; Carbs: 33g; Protein: 4g

Baked Stuffed Apples

Preparation time: 10 minutes
Cooking time: 15 minutes
Servings: 4

Ingredients:
- 4 apples, cut the top off & scoop out the flesh from the centre
- 6 tsp raisins
- 2 tsp chopped walnuts
- 2 tsp honey
- .50 tsp cinnamon

Directions:
1. Stuff the apples with raisins, walnuts, honey and cinnamon. Divide these apples into the two air fryer baskets.
2. Place both baskets in your air fryer. Choose "AIR FRY" for the first basket at 177°C and set the time to 15 minutes.
3. Choose the "MATCH COOK" for second basket, and press the "START/PAUSE" to start cooking. Serve!

Nutrition: Calories: 175; Fat: 13g; Carbs: 14g; Protein: 0g

Brownie Muffins

Preparation time: 10 minutes
Cooking time: 15 minutes
Servings: 10 muffins

Ingredients:
- 2 eggs
- 96g all-purpose flour
- 1 tsp vanilla
- 130g powdered sugar
- 25g cocoa powder
- 37g pecans, chopped
- 1 tsp cinnamon
- 113g butter, melted

Directions:
1. Whisk the eggs, vanilla, butter, sugar, and cinnamon in a bowl until well-mixed. Add the cocoa powder and flour and stir until well combined.
2. Add the pecans and fold well. Pour batter into the silicone muffin moulds.
3. Insert a crisper plate in air fryer baskets. Place muffin moulds in both baskets.
4. Place both baskets in your air fryer. Choose "BAKE" for the first basket at 182°C and set the time to 15 minutes.
5. Choose the "MATCH COOK" for second basket, and press the "START/PAUSE" to start cooking. Serve!

Nutrition: Calories: 210; Fat: 10g; Carbs: 28g; Protein: 3g

Scottish Shortbread Sticks

Preparation time: 15 minutes
Cooking time: 18 minutes
Servings: 1 dozen cookies

Ingredients:
- 113g butter, softened
- 43g packed brown sugar
- 120g all-purpose flour

Directions:
1. Whisk the softened butter plus sugar in your bowl until frothy. Add the flour and mix well until you have a dough.
2. Knead your dough for 5-8 minutes in clean floured surface. Roll it out and slice it into sticks.
3. Divide the sticks into two air fryer baskets with the crisper plate installed. Choose "BAKE" for the first basket at 176°C and set the time to 18 minutes.
4. Choose the "MATCH COOK" for second basket and press the "START/PAUSE" to start cooking. Let it cool and serve.

Nutrition: Calories: 193; Fat: 11g; Carbs: 21g; Protein: 1g

Honey Lime Pineapple

Preparation time: 10 minutes + chilling time
Cooking time: 10 minutes
Servings: 4

Ingredients:
- 562g pineapple chunks
- 55g brown sugar
- 30ml lime juice
- 63g honey

Directions:
1. Mix the pineapple, honey, lime juice, and brown sugar in a bowl. Cover and place in refrigerator for 1 hour.
2. Insert a crisper plate in air fryer baskets. Remove the pineapple chunks from the marinade and place them in both baskets.
3. Place both baskets in your air fryer. Choose "AIR FRY" for the first basket at 199°C and set the time to 10 minutes.
4. Choose the "MATCH COOK" for second basket, and press the "START/PAUSE" to start cooking. Stir halfway through. Serve!

Nutrition: Calories: 153; Fat: 0g; Carbs: 40g; Protein: 0g

Chocó Lava Cake

Preparation time: 10 minutes
Cooking time: 10 minutes
Servings: 4

Ingredients:
- 3 eggs
- 3 egg yolks
- 70g dark chocolate, chopped
- 168g cups powdered sugar
- 96g all-purpose flour
- 1 tsp vanilla
- 113g butter

- .50 tsp salt

Directions:
1. Add the chocolate and butter to a bowl and microwave for 30 seconds. Remove from microwave and stir until smooth.
2. Add the eggs, egg yolks, sugar, flour, vanilla, and salt into the melted chocolate, then stir until well combined. Pour the batter into the four greased ramekins.
3. Insert a crisper plate in air fryer baskets. Place the ramekins in both baskets.
4. Place both baskets in your air fryer. Choose "AIR FRY" for the first basket at 199°C and set the time to 10 minutes.
5. Choose the "MATCH COOK" for second basket, and press the "START/PAUSE" to start cooking. Serve!

Nutrition: Calories: 387; Fat: 37g; Carbs: 28g; Protein: 10g

COOKING CONVERSION CHART

Volume Equivalents (Liquid)

US STANDARD	US STANDARD (OUNCES)	METRIC (APPROXIMATE)
2 tablespoons	1 fl. oz.	30 mL
¼ cup	2 fl. oz.	60 mL
½ cup	4 fl. oz.	120 mL
1 cup	8 fl. oz.	240 mL
1½ cups	12 fl. oz.	355 mL
2 cups or 1 pint	16 fl. oz.	475 mL
4 cups or 1 quart	32 fl. oz.	1 L
1 gallon	128 fl. oz.	4 L

Volume Equivalents (Dry)

US STANDARD	METRIC (APPROXIMATE)
⅛ teaspoon	0.5 mL
¼ teaspoon	1 mL
½ teaspoon	2 mL
¾ teaspoon	4 mL
1 teaspoon	5 mL
1 tablespoon	15 mL
¼ cup	59 mL
⅓ cup	79 mL
½ cup	118 mL
⅔ cup	156 mL
¾ cup	177 mL
1 cup	235 mL
2 cups or 1 pint	475 mL
3 cups	700 mL
4 cups or 1 quart	1 L
½ gallon	2 L
1 gallon	4 L

Weight Equivalents

US STANDARD	METRIC (APPROXIMATE)
½ ounce	15 g
1 ounce	30 g
2 ounces	60 g
4 ounces	115 g
8 ounces	225 g
12 ounces	340 g
16 ounces or 1 pound	455 g

Conclusion

The Dual Zone Air Fryer is the next big thing in air frying. No matter how unbelievable the concept might sound, the people behind this amazing Dual Zone Air Fryer has put on countless hours of engineering into crafting this meticulously designed appliance that takes the Air Frying game to a whole different level.

At its heart, the Dual Zone Air Fryer is two air fryers in one appliance. This means that you can cook two different foods at once, each in its own cooking zone. The two zones are separated by a physical divider, so there's no chance of the flavours mixing. It's also big enough to cook a meal for the whole family. With a 4-quart capacity in each zone, you can cook up to 8 servings at once.

While handling two Air Fryer baskets might sound a little bit complicated at first, the way how Kitchen has engineered this appliance has made it extremely accessible and easy to handle.

And we hope this cookbook has given you a great foundation to start your journey with the Dual Zone Air Fryer. There are countless recipes and possibilities with this appliance, and we hope this cookbook has helped open your eyes to some of them. While the recipes in this cookbook are a great starting point, we encourage you to get creative in the kitchen and come up with your own unique creations. So, get creative, and have fun!

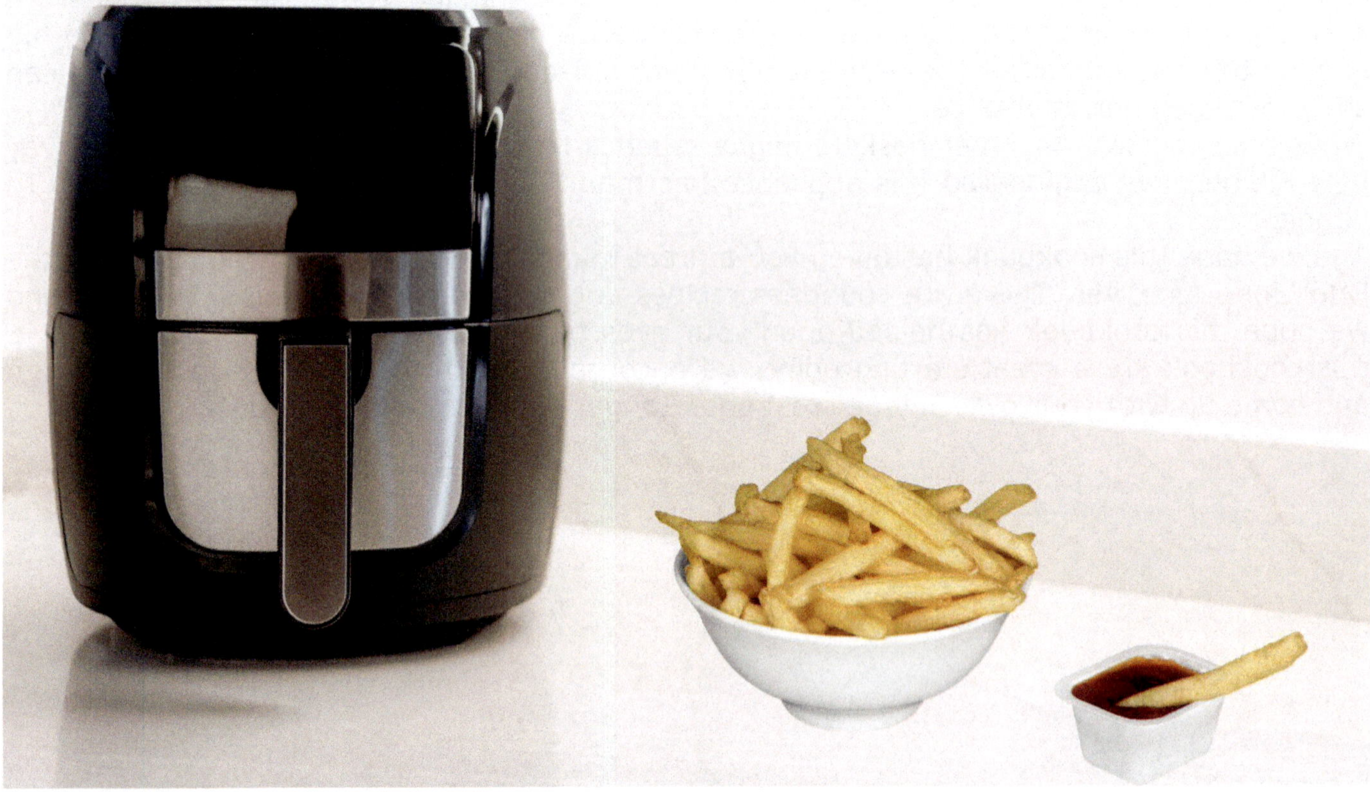